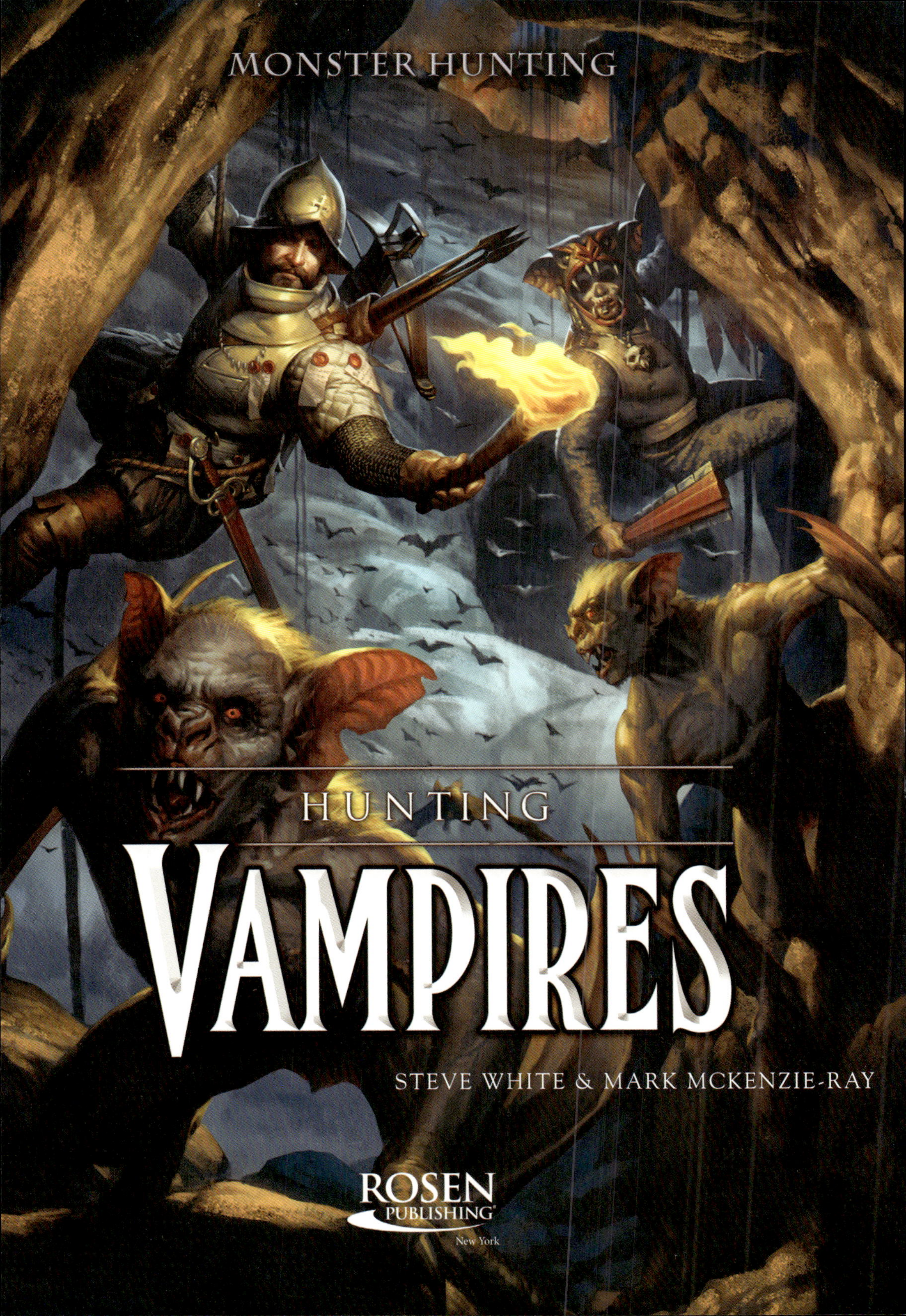

MONSTER HUNTING

HUNTING VAMPIRES

STEVE WHITE & MARK MCKENZIE-RAY

ROSEN PUBLISHING
New York

This edition published in 2017 by
The Rosen Publishing Group, Inc.
29 East 21st Street
New York, NY 10010

Library of Congress Cataloging-in-Publication Data

Names: White, Steve, 1964– author.
Title: Hunting vampires / Steve White and Mark Mckenzie-Ray.
Description: New York : Rosen Publishing, 2017. | Series: Monster hunting | Includes bibliographical references and index.
Identifiers: LCCN 2016039087 | ISBN 9781499465303 (library bound)
Subjects: LCSH: Vampires.
Classification: LCC BF1556 .W48 2016 | DDC 398/.45—dc23
LC record available at https://lccn.loc.gov/2016039087

Manufactured in the United States of America

Contents

Introduction

From the highly regarded classic to the downright ridiculous, vampire stories have fascinated humanity for centuries. But is there more to these narratives than poetic license? Similarities in the depiction of the creatures and their behavior within these texts is clearly evident, and real-world reports of vampire-related events have contributed to the cultural history of almost every continent in the world, be it through oral retelling or actual documentation.

There has been little respect for studies into the existence of vampires, a creature that is long considered to have been a product of superstition, given life by the whispers of legend and folklore. The authors of this guide are great admirers of vampires and have spent many nights researching and documenting vampire species from around the globe. In fact, it was during our own separate lines of research that we first crossed paths. From the moment we began debating Séan Manchester's theories put forward for the case of the Highgate vampire incidents from the 1970s, we knew we had found a kindred spirit in one another.

Our work attracted the attention of the United Nations Educational, Scientific & Cultural Organization (UNESCO) – a United Nations agency that sponsors programs in arts, communication and culture. UNESCO had been playing close attention to our research as we delved headfirst into the vampire underworld. We saw the worst the species had to offer during our time behind the front lines. We wanted to understand the creatures better: where do they come from? What is their motivation? Are they merely victims of scapegoating? The information our research has uncovered is both fascinating and alarming.

During our work with UNESCO, the organization was able to confirm one startling piece of information that the authors had long suspected: hunters the world over have been independently fighting vampires for millennia. Until now, their activities had stayed mostly hidden and the vampire threat was kept relatively under control. But now the underworld is a hive of activity as the "undead" prepare to assemble their forces and rise up against humanity.

UNESCO is reacting by aggressively stepping up the recruitment and training of its own counter-units. Vampire hunters are being deployed across the globe to fight the massing hordes of vampires. Dubbed SAU (Special Action Units), these groups are using every piece of information at their disposal to neutralize the growing threat.

What we have compiled is a handbook of sorts: a basic background to the vampires, drawing on information that we have gathered through our research and first-hand experience with these deadly and uncompromising creatures. Within these pages, you will find explanations of a number of vampires in areas across five continents: Europe, North America, Africa, Asia and South America. We have focused our content on a select number of vampire subspecies – those that present the biggest threats to humanity now and in the foreseeable future – within the three principal classes of vampire: haemophages (blood drinkers), psychics, and a combination of the two.

Studying our targets' origins will allow a greater understanding of their behavior and motivations. We reach far back into prehistory, beyond even the first recorded mention of the creatures in the Russian *Primary Chronicle* (1047), a historical text that features a Novogorodian priest known as Upyr' Likhij (Wicked Vampire). Though the Slavic origin of the "vampire" has established Europe as a hotbed of vampiric activity for more than a thousand

Strigoi, the classic European vampires, are extremely difficult to photograph. Not only do they generally not want their pictures taken, but their images seem to slide off film in a way not completely understood to science. This situation has somewhat improved with the rise of digital photography, but authentic photographs of vampires remain a rarity.

years, our research proves that the reach of the vampire is far greater than we could have ever imagined.

No guide to vampire hunting would be complete without an analysis of the methods used to destroy the enemy. As each vampire has evolved in its surroundings, hunters have retaliated by adapting their skills and techniques to take on the threats in their locale. The comprehensive examination of each hunter, from their humble beginnings to their current practices and successes, is told with a view to inform. Today's vampire hunters should look to the styles that follow to influence their own methods as they prepare to fight every type of vampire, as more and more species migrate from their native countries to integrate themselves into foreign covens. A new, global empire is on the horizon, one that will threaten the existence of the human species as we know it.

Our studies have been prepared to arm any potential vampire hunter with the knowledge required to support their training and become skilled in their profession. Forget everything you thought you knew about vampires – your education starts right here.

A still from the 1922 silent film, *Nosferatu*. After a legal battle involving the Bram Stoker estate, all copies of the film were ordered destroyed by the German courts. Thankfully one copy survived this purge. Many have interpreted the incident as an effort by European vampires to suppress knowledge of their existence. (Pictorial Press Ltd / Alamy)

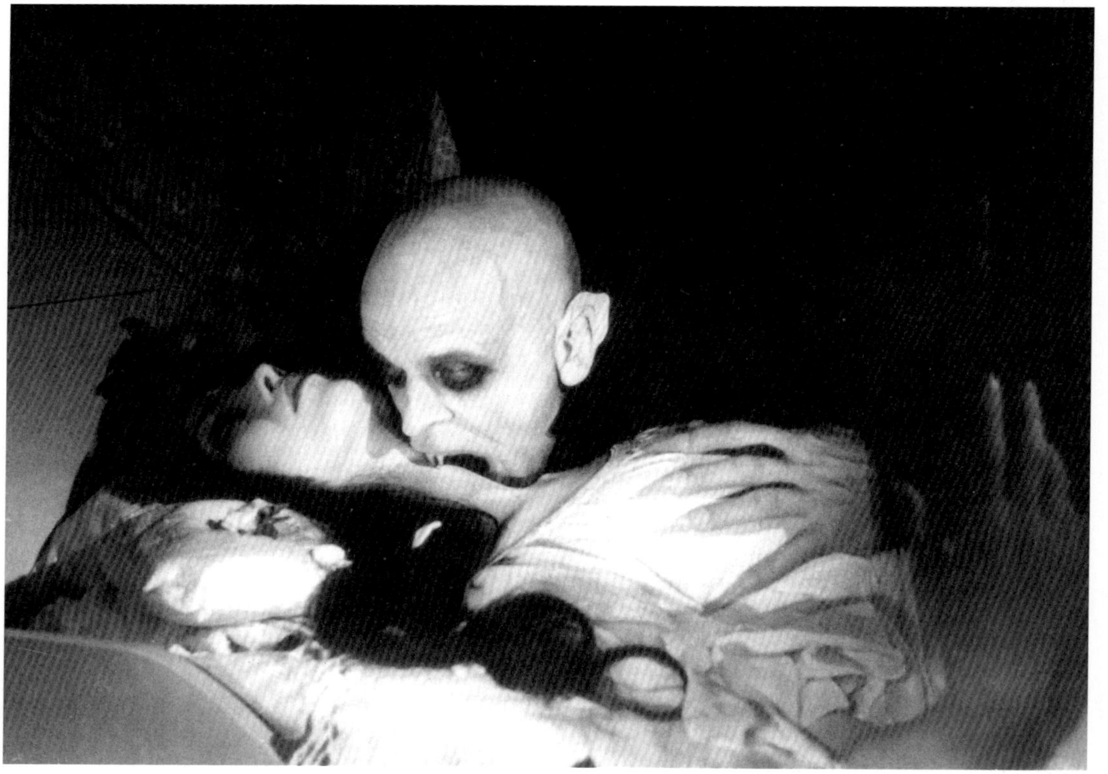

Chapter 1 – THE SAU IN ACTION

At dusk on the evening of September 13, 1995, an unusual religious service was held in the chapel of the UNPROFOR (United Nations Protection Force) base at Divilji Barracks, in Split, Croatia. Operation *Deliberate Force*, the UN's belated response to the siege of Sarajevo and the atrocities being committed by Serb forces in Bosnia, was two days old.

Gathered in the chapel were a dozen men and women from as many nations; the Catholic priest now blessing them had heard their confessions and was now saying Mass for the group who, to any outsider, might have looked like Special Forces operatives or private security contractors. They had no definitive uniform, other than that they all wore black and crucifixes hung around their necks. Piled by the door were their UN-issue blue helmets and their weapons: automatic shotguns and high-powered assault rifles, all low-velocity types. Clearly, whatever ammunition they fired was intended to stay in the target. Each gun carried a torch, at first glance apparently white light or infrared, but all actually ultra-violet.

Closer inspection would also have revealed that the body armor they wore was acid-etched with Biblical inscriptions in Latin and Serbo-Croat, and religious iconography was subtly worked into the metal and ceramics. Their weapons also held unusual ammunition. The shotgun rounds fired flechettes of consecrated, carbonized wood or ball-bearings of silver, also blessed. The assault rifles, all 7.62mm caliber, used silver or carbon graphite slugs converted to illegal dum-dums.

Just after midnight, the team of the innocuously named First Special Action Unit climbed aboard two British Army Lynx helicopters, part of the Heli Ops flight based at Split. It could have been carrying an SAS unit out on a night insertion, and was a pretty regular sight at Split. The blue UN helmets were still in the chapel when the Lynx took off and headed off into the dark. Air attacks were under way across Bosnia, and the Lynx flight was just two aircraft amongst dozens on the move that night.

They headed towards the Dinaric Alps that ran next to the Adriatic Sea, along the Croatian coast. Flying just above the treetops, the Lynx flight was heading towards a hidden cave deep within the rugged mountain chain.

The 1st SAU's (nicknamed "saw") mission had begun the week before – the actual dates and times remain largely classified. The unit had inserted itself into the UNPROFOR base with ease. Many nations had contingents at

This shot of unmarked Black Hawk helicopters is thought to be the only photographic evidence of SAU activity in Bosnia. (US Department of Defense)

the base and new faces came and went with monotonous frequency. There was a veritable bazar of uniform types. It was easy for those on missions of questionable veracity to come and go. The SAU's mission was one known to very few select members of the UN mission and NATO high command, and a few government officials. The unit received the most classified intelligence but also had access to the very latest reconnaissance imagery from across the war-torn region. But it also drew information from all manner of sources. The unit looked at raw news footage and reports from journalists throughout the war zone, from Special Forces patrols, UN inspectors and aerial reconnaissance interpretation units. They even interviewed prisoners of war and defectors. And if anyone asked why – and they rarely did – they were gathering evidence for war crimes tribunals.

But their real target was something far more deadly, the Strigoi.

Centuries of hunters had made the Strigoi rare in their home territories. However, the breakup of Yugoslavia changed that. As Croatia, Serbia and Bosnia fractured and the specter of ethnic cleansing fell upon the region, reports began to emerge of renewed activity by the Strigoi. No longer capable of lording it over terrified peasantry, their castles had long since fallen to ruin and their mausoleums had been destroyed by terrified locals. Their lairs remained undetected, but as the situation in the Balkans degenerated, rumors began to circulate that not all of the killing could be attributed to the work of frenzied paramilitaries or genocidal militias killing unfortunate Muslims. It seems the Strigoi initially tried to cover up their activities by burning their victims, but UN pathologists exhuming a grave in northern Bosnia found the dead to be exsanguinated. The report was initially attributed to some kind of ritualistic behavior by a guerrilla unit and largely ignored, but it piqued the interest of regional vampire hunters. Word spread throughout the hunting community and officials at the UN began investigating in earnest.

As the situation around Sarajevo worsened in the summer of 1995, the first real signs of Strigoi activity appeared (and were subsequently classified and obfuscated). Mass killings hinted that the vampires, after decades – even centuries – of isolation and near-extinction, and with so much real killing going on to hide their own appetites, found themselves like foxes in a hencoop. They killed without restraint. A UN vehicle patrol near Tuzla in August 1995 found a busload of women and children killed. There was no attempt to hide the bodies, which had clearly been exsanguinated. There was nothing organized in the butchery, nothing to suggest an execution. It was enough to bring real fear to the locals, while the UN troops (from Holland) were immediately transferred out of the region to stop any rumors spreading. UN special pathologists arrived on the scene the following night and treated the bodies of the dead (using decapitation and cardiac puncture), which were then cremated.

The Strigoi's lack of finesse eventually gave them away. A shepherd boy had discovered what appeared to be a new cave system high in the Dinaric Alps. He also reported seeing large, red-furred bats. A UNESCO science team, ignoring the situation in the region, decided to investigate, hoping the boy might have discovered caves similar to the Movile system in Romania, with its unique groundwater ecosystem.

A photographic reconstruction of one of the Strigoi encountered by SAU agents during their mission of September 13, 1995.

Two days after arriving at the caves, and after some exciting initial finds, the team reported seeing a beautiful, red-haired woman watching them from the cave. That night, the boy guide vanished. By the following day, contact with the team had ceased. The general conclusion was that they had been kidnapped, or worse.

In Split, the SAU followed the reports with interest. Under the guise of investigating the disappearance, the SAU launched their mission of September 13.

After rappelling into the ravine from the helicopters, the team used night-vision goggles (NVGs) to negotiate their way to the cave entrance. There was a strong smell of ammonia. Prepared for such an eventuality, they put on gas masks and entered the cave.

Deep inside, they discovered a massive bat colony. The conditions could only be described as hellish. Huge dunes of guano (which rained down constantly from the roosting bats in the cave roof) were covered in a seething mass of cockroaches and other bugs. The smell was appalling and the constant flittering of the bats cluttered the NVGs, drawing light from the bioluminescence emanating from the rotting dung.

Struggling up the guano dunes and further into the caves, the SAU had their first inclination of something amiss when one of the team spotted a large, red-furred bat overhead. When it was hit by a beam of UV torchlight, it emitted an incredibly high-pitched scream.

Shortly after, the SAU was attacked.

Corroborated reports tell us what happened in those caves. Harpy-like Strigoaică (female Strogoi) descended out of nowhere, and in seconds at least two SAU members were dead. The roar of gunfire echoing around the caves stirred up the bats, who took to the air in a whirlwind of wings. Chaos ensued and the team were forced to retire, but not before at least two Strigoaică were hit by fire. One lay screaming and flapping, her wing shredded by a flechette round. One of the team shot her in the chest and throat with silver shotgun rounds. A second was blasted out of the air by a shot to the chest, which vaporized under a storm of wooden darts.

In disarray, the team made it out of the cave, but five were dead and three were injured – one by friendly fire, hit in the shoulder by silver shotgun pellets. The others were scratched but none bitten.

Evacuated by the helicopters, the survivors called down fire from an orbiting AC-130H Spectre gunship operating with the 16th Special Operations Group out of Brindisi. Cannon fire collapsed the entrance of the cave but it remains unknown if any of the Strigoi escaped. To be certain that the entrance remained properly sealed, two Tomahawk cruise missiles were fired from the guided-missile cruiser, the USS *Normandy*, into the cave entrance, their huge 1,000lb warheads bringing the cave and surrounding ravine crashing down.

The hunt was now on for any Strigoi who may have fled the battle, while the SAU retired to lick its wounds.

The USS *Normandy*, which fired the final shots (a pair of Tomahawk cruise missiles) during the September 13, 1995 mission. (US Department of Defense)

Chapter 2 - European Vampires

Early History of the Strigoi

The fear of returning from the dead dates back to prehistory, and if there was ever a geographical center for that fear, it was Europe. In an Iron Age site in Bavaria, a violently killed woman was buried beneath a large stone, presumably to keep her from rising from her grave.

Ancient Greece was an early home of the vampire legend. Empusa was the demonic daughter of the goddess Hecate, herself often associated with witchcraft, magic and crossroads. Empusa drank the blood of men she seduced as a beautiful young woman. Another goddess, Lamia, drained young children in revenge for the killing of her own infants by Zeus' wife, Hera, after the latter discovered Lamia's affair with her husband.

Despite their apparently unnatural origins, the first vampires were still limited by certain laws of nature. As a "top predator," their numbers remained small and they were limited by slow reproductive rates, whether via actually breeding or by the "turning" of victims. Even so, around the Carpathians and eastern Alps, vampires became an increasing hazard for the local population.

It was in the first few centuries BCE, and largely through the Christianization of the region, that the first countermeasures were developed against these first "true" vampires, now known as the Strigoi. Hunters used to dealing with wolves and bears refined methods to kill vampires that were initially fairly straightforward: beheading, burning and staking, often all three.

However, with the region's population becoming more firmly Christian in the following centuries, it seems the first amuletic defences started to become common. Studies indicate that this use of religious symbols to ward off vampires may have arisen as a result of local Christians being turned into vampires. Devoted in their beliefs, it is possible that these victims felt themselves cursed or demonized, and as such vulnerable to Christian symbols such as the cross and holy water. These beliefs could have been psychosomatically very powerful, to the extent that they took on actual physical manifestations, and if the vampires' beliefs were powerful enough it was passed on culturally within the colony. As such, a psychological belief became an instinctive one, possibly passed on at an almost genetic level.

It was also during the 5th and 6th centuries that the first warrior priests appeared. They were trained in local monasteries, but as boys were already

TYPES OF STRIGOI

Like many top predators, the Strigoi have cultures adapted to specialist prey. This has led to the rise in a belief that there are a number of different European vampire types. Actually, they are all now believed to be the same species of the Strigoi vampire, and are found throughout Europe.

Pijavica: a Strigoi particular to the Balkans and Czech Republic.

Shtriga: An Albanian variation that lacks the usual beautiful female appearance and is instead hideous or demonic, or like an ancient crone. However, they still favor the blood of infants. Reports claim that a Shtriga can prevent the turning of her victim by spitting in their mouth. This has been interpreted as a possible natural "antivenom" contained within the Shtriga, and efforts are under way by SAU to capture one of these particular specimens. They are thought to be vulnerable to garlic and pig-bone crosses.

Vjesci: A Polish species recognized by a caul (lump) on their forehead. Removal of the lump on the seventh birthday of the victim prevents "turning" (a significant date similar to the life cycle of the cambion, a product of human/vampire procreation). It is reported that they are susceptible to religious icons.

Mullo (Muli = male; Mulo = female): Romany/gypsy variation; considered a person to have died of wrongful or unnatural causes, or for whom the correct funeral rites were not observed. They have a propensity for poltergeist-like behavior, often vindictive or vengeful. This behavior is often focused around family members or those whom the Mullo had a particular grievance against in life.

They also seem to be afflicted with a physical abnormality that varies from individual to individual (a clawed foot or hand, the beginnings of a tail) and are often of hideous appearance. A possible explanation for this is that the transformation to a "true" vampire has failed or been interrupted, perhaps due to some genetic trait or medical condition. It is interesting to note that Mullo rise any time between 40 days and five years after death, which, compared to other Strigoi that rise within hours, indicates some abnormality in the transformation process.

However, the Mullo does retain a relatively "human" state and, as such, they are unable to sire new Mullo but can impregnate human females, resulting in hybrid offspring known as Dhampirs.

This incomplete transformation might also explain the Mullo's attachment to its family and memory of its previous existence.

Romany methods of disposal are variations on regular methods: metal pins or needles inserted into the heart, mouth, eyes, ears and between the fingers, and hawthorn stakes driven into the legs.

well versed in the art of hunting wolves and bears, and with a deep-rooted familiarity with the surrounding landscape. As such, they knew the likely hideouts of vampires, be it a cave system or an abandoned farmstead, and how to track them to their lair. For the first time since prehistory, humanity was taking the fight to the vampires that they had named the Strigoi.

Despite this, the warrior priests were few and far between. It was also a difficult region in which to hunt, a wilderness of high mountains and deep forests, with a multitude of hiding places from which the Strigoi could strike. Because of this, in their Eastern European homelands the vampires went largely unchallenged throughout their early history.

The Middle Ages

It was not until the time of the First Crusade that any organized defense against the Strigoi and their kin first appeared.

Following the call of Pope Urban II at the Council of Clermont in France in November 1095, the First Crusade gathered largely under the auspices of saving the Byzantine Empire from the apparent threat of a Muslim invasion. While the armies of Europe gathered their forces, a rather less disciplined and rag-tag Crusade took up Urban's call and set off for the Holy Land. With few knights amongst its ranks, the army was largely composed of poor and illiterate peasants, many hoping for a new life and wealth in the east.

In August 1096, the "People's Crusade" as it was known, swept through Eastern Europe like a locust plague. Poorly equipped and hungry, these "crusaders" sacked any town that could not resist them, be it Christian or not, even doing battle with Hungarian forces when they began to starve.

The People's Crusade was an unexpected boon for the Strigoi. The poorly armed, disorganized, ignorant peasants provided rich picking for the vampires as they passed through the region. Lost and hungry groups of travelers blundered into the Carpathians and

Although there are very few written records of vampires from the Middle Ages, depictions of them can be found in artwork and sculptures, such as this grotesque from a Spanish cathedral. (PD)

were quickly annihilated, swelling the number of Strigoi and making them confident enough to leave their usual hunting grounds to haunt the peasant crusaders, picking off stragglers and the weak.

The People's Crusade reached Constantinople, the capital of the Byzantine Empire, in late August and immediately caused enough trouble that the city closed its gates to the peasants. They were, however, quickly offered boats across the Bosporus into the Levant, where they were very soon massacred by local Muslim forces.

Blood Libel

The preaching of the Crusade had a horrific impact on European Jews, who many Christians saw as equally the enemies of Christ as the Muslims. By the end of 1095, pogroms had begun in France and Germany, even though violence against the Jews was never sanctioned by the Christian leadership, which was much more intent on converting them.

The first *milites Christi* ("soldiers of Christ") entered the region at the end of the 11th century. Many were educated monks and listened to the local stories of vampires with interest, immediately recognizing (with their own skewed vision) the hand of Satan at work. To them, the Strigoi were nothing less than demons from hell and, interested in seeing the vampires for themselves, they organized the first vampire pogroms, or anti-vampire uprisings. The newly confident Strigoi were suddenly confronted with righteous, well-equipped and confident knights, many battle-hardened from years of fighting in Europe. Despite their natural attributes, the vampires were driven back into the mountains and forests, and vanished back underground into their caves and sarcophagi.

The Malthusian Dilemma

The Strigoi and humanity reached something of an impasse during the 12th and 13th centuries. The vampires restricted themselves to the shadows amidst the wilderness of Eastern Europe, their numbers stabilizing while they held sway over the peasant populations scratching out a living as sheep farmers on the surrounding hills and forests. As time passed, the theological nature of defense against the Strigoi solidified and the first "vampires" began to hold court in (ironically) abandoned monasteries and castles.

Meanwhile, the *milites Christi* were busy elsewhere battling Saracens and Cathars. They even, in some cases, turned on their own, when at the start of the 14th century the Knights Templar were destroyed by Philip IV of France, eager to get his hands on their treasury.

By the middle of the 14th century, Europe's human population had reached a point where the number of people now outstripped available resources – a Malthusian dilemma. A series of harsh summers and terrible winters in the early decades of the 1300s triggered crop failures and starvation. This caused a backlash of wars, social unrest and the rise of apocalyptic superstition. This culminated in the Black Death.

Arriving with the Mongols during their advance west from the steppes of the Gobi Desert, bubonic plague spread from Italy to the north of England in just over 1,000 days. Human populations, weakened by perennial hunger, proved highly vulnerable to the plague. Twenty-five million people perished, up to 60 percent of Europe's population.

It was only natural for many to believe that the end of days had arrived.

For the Strigoi, the collapse of social order around them left the survivors wide open to attack. Immune to the plague bacteria, they once more left the forests and mountains and descended on villages and towns in unprecedented numbers. For the people struggling to survive the horrors of the plague and coming to terms with the sense of abandonment by God, the arrival of the vampires must have seemed to have been the final, sure sign that the end was indeed nigh.

The Strigoi reclaimed many of their old hunting grounds, and for about a century, they seemed invulnerable. Colonies established themselves throughout the Carpathian region, dominating the surrounding areas and even triggering the supplying of sacrifices to certain Strigoi mort (male Strigoi) to ward off their worst excesses.

Although the depiction of the vampire as a skeleton is inaccurate, this drawing demonstrates two effective methods of vampire elimination, staking and fire. (Mary Evans Picture Library / Alamy)

However, the Strigoi had overextended themselves. By the start of the 15th century, the crash in the human population had begun to have a marked impact on the vampires, whose own numbers had begun to collapse as they exhausted their supply of "livestock." The few travelers that braved the wilderness regions of Eastern Europe reported abandoned villages, towns with a few hardy but perpetually terrified locals who never moved at night, and the sound of terrifying battles emanating from high Alpine forests and distant ravines. The latter is believed to have been territorial wars between vampire colonies as many were displaced when their food supplies became exhausted and they were forced into the territory of a neighboring clan. The result, in any case, was that the Strigoi found themselves victims of their own success.

The Inquisition

In 1478, the Spanish formed their infamous Inquisition to maintain Christian (Catholic) orthodoxy in the face of increasing heretical forces. By now, Jews, Muslims and Cathars had been joined by Protestants. There was also a growing anxiety concerning witchcraft and devil worship throughout a Europe that was still recovering from the bacterial carnage of the Black Death. The result was that the *milites Christi* began to organize once more, in one form or another, feeding the mounting hysteria that was to sweep through all parts of Europe. This led ultimately to the auto-da-fé and witch trials that killed so many, as warrior knights and judges took their responsibilities far beyond their original intentions.

In the light of these developments, in 1520 a papal bull led to the organization of the first Vatican-sanctioned inquisition into the threat posed by vampires. This was a minor bureaucratic and administrative event, overshadowed as it was by the coming hundred years of religious wars about to rend Europe, but for the Strigoi it was like the coming of their own Black Death.

Initially, *milites Christi* soldier-scholars combed reports of vampire activity simply to prove the threat existed. However, when this proved inconclusive and largely apocryphal, a punitive expedition into the Carpathian region was mounted in 1528.

By this point, the Strigoi population was a pale shadow of its former self, and the few local human populations were by now tough and well versed in combating the vampire menace. Their amuletic defenses were also well and truly developed, and the Vatican *milites Christi* were only too happy to use such tried and tested methods.

However, as the locals were content to tough it out in the shadow of the vampires, so the surviving vampires had made it through very difficult times and learned a few tricks of their own. Many were centuries old and had long

(Opposite) A depiction of the famous vampire hunter, Pieter Van Sloan, who many credit as the inspiration for Bram Stoker's character Abraham Van Helsing. Van Sloan operated all over the European mainland in the second half of the 19th century, before disappearing in Bavaria in 1882.

abandoned any fear of religious or hallowed weapons. As such, when the *milites Christi* ascended into the Carpathians seeking to engage the vampires, the first battles proved inconclusive and set a precedent that was to remain largely unchanged into modern times. The numbers of Strigoi were held in check by the organized forces dedicated to their destruction; meanwhile, the older vampires, hardened by decades, even centuries, of battling for their very survival were very hard to kill, and remained locally powerful.

A status quo developed, and from their lairs, manmade or otherwise, these vampires passed into legend – or across the Atlantic, as some of the more wealthy and powerful Strigoi mort sought new and safer hunting grounds.

Yet the vampire myth continued to permeate history, even outliving the Renaissance and the Enlightenment, when many superstitions and folklores were refuted. But still the Strigoi lingered on, especially in Eastern Europe, where the sparse and largely illiterate population made easy prey for venerable and wily vampires. It was only in the 19th century, as the region developed and populations swelled, that the Strigoi found themselves once more being burned out of their ancestral resting places. Ironically, in Western Europe, this was the period when, largely as a result of Bram Stoker's *Dracula*, the vampire took on its romantic, mystical allure.

At this point, it is probably worth pointing out that the inspiration for Stoker's Dracula, Vlad the Impaler, was nothing but a man. He masqueraded as a vampire, but was probably nothing more than a megalomaniacal sadist who was clinically psychotic and used the legends and myths of the vampire to heighten a reputation built on fear. But to the Strigoi, nailing hats to heads and impaling prisoners was seen as laughable, the actions of a child burning ants with a magnifying glass.

Since Shtriga vampires are thought to have some kind of vampiric antivenom glands in their throat or mouth, there is currently a large bounty on their heads. (Reconstruction by Hauke Kock)

Strigoi Field Guide

The Strigoi are the classical European haemophage, the creature that most people in Western society think of when they hear the term "vampire." Sometimes identified by the classical form "vampire," they are (or were) particularly numerous in Eastern Europe and the Balkans, but nests or covens can be found in most countries. In the overpopulated 21st century, small communities find it easy to hide in the anonymity and multiculturalism of major cities and amongst the mass migrations of urban populations. This hiding in plain sight conversely makes them very hard to track and hunt.

Strigoi can be identified by their pale, white, almost translucent skin and red-rimmed eyes. They are almost always "beautiful" or "handsome" in appearance. They are also mostly female (known as Strigoaică). They are often thought to be witches, or *stryge* (French for "bird-woman"). The confusion seems to have arisen from the Strigoaică's ability to transform into large bats. Some are also able to transform into wolves. They are also famous for their long red hair, giving their human forms a striking beauty, useful in luring eager young men to their death (although they prefer children). Finally, they can "turn" or "sire" victims, creating new Strigoi by passing on their own blood to the victim, who takes on an undead state post-mortem.

The male Strigoi (Strigoi mort) are more powerful, almost demonic in their capabilities. They have a mesmerizing allure and, while the fact that this is somehow psychic has already been mentioned, research hints at a powerful pheromone as the source of this. The Strigoi mort is often portrayed as having a particular interest in young women, but it could be rather more prosaic than that; the immature young are simply easier and more suggestible as prey. Male Strigoi are generally very strong and very fast.

Though it is rare, some vampires are turned while still children. These child vampires or Ustrel have a propensity for killing livestock, but this is now thought to be merely practice; it is also easier to hide an attack on a cow or pig by blaming bear or wolf attack. As it becomes more skilled, the Ustrel begins taking human prey. However, even amongst Strigoi, the turning of children is seen as cruel and generally avoided.

For most of European history, hunters have relied on religious amuletic defenses and wooden stakes to take down vampires. Today, their weapons are much more hi-tech.

All Strigoi, male, female or children, are more vulnerable in their first 30 years as a vampire. During this time, they cannot stand sunlight, must sleep on a bed of their native soil and are only marginally faster and stronger than humans. However, around the age of 30, Strigoi develop into Kukudhi, their adulthood. With this age comes strength, exaggerated reflexes, and fully developed vampiric powers including mesmerism, psychokinesis, telepathy, a resistance to amuletic attack, and zoomutation, especially into bat, wolf or dog-like forms.

Siring

The creation of a new Strigoi is called "siring" or "turning" and requires blood transfusions between both parties, the most significant being ingestion of the sire's blood by the victim (although "sire" is generally a masculine term, here it refers to both male and female).

After this event, the victim's body suffers a catastrophic shutdown of all major functions, leading ultimately to a comatose state that could easily be perceived as death. In this state of medical hibernation, the vampiric vector (possibly a virus delivered by the Strigoi's fangs, although this has yet to be isolated) begins its radical restructuring of the victim's major organs and systems down to a genetic level. The skin becomes little more than a chrysalis or pupae, the organs degenerating to a pulp or liquid as they reorganize.

Strigoi rise quickly after being turned, sometimes within just a few hours, but usually within a day. This takes an enormous amount of energy, which is why new Strigoi awake from this comatose state ravenous and quick to make easy kills, although they are often clumsy and obviously inexperienced. As such, the sire is usually on hand to help the new vampire through the difficult transition period, the changes being not only physical and behavioral, but psychological as well. This combination makes new vampires very vulnerable.

Reproduction

The Strigoi generally procreate by turning human adults. However, the Romanian vampire known as the Morai (Moroaică is the female) raises interesting questions about Strigoi reproduction. Traditionally more closely related to werewolves and lycanthropy, recent studies indicate Morai are actually the children of two Strigoi. By and large, Strigoi are sterile; conception is a rare event. Culturally, the Strigoi see such offspring as abominations; they are unusual in being "mortal," i.e. they have the same lifespan as a normal human.

Moreover, the blood of Morai is much sought after by Strigoi for its apparent potency, and even without their "mortal" lifespans, few Morai survive to anything like adulthood. (They also make fine bait for SAU ambushes.)

Morai are also said to be vulnerable to wolf attack and tame wolves are often used to hunt these unfortunate vampires.

Strigoi Vulnerabilities and Termination

Prior to developing into a Kukudhi, a Strigoi is required to sleep in native soil, either in its original coffin or in a vessel filled with the necessary earth, during the hours of daylight. This limits their movements and, if the location of their resting place can be determined, makes them vulnerable to ambush. More experienced Strigoi will have cached native soil in various locations to broaden the scope of their movements.

Romanian hunters demonstrating that there is no such thing as overkill when dealing with the undead. Note the size of hammer that was presumably used to drive the stake into the heart. Driving wood through a human chest is harder than most people realize. (Historical image collection by Bildagentur-online / Alamy)

Like any top predator, after a good meal Strigoi can become listless and slow-moving; caught in the open, away from their resting place, they are far easier to engage.

The Strigoi can, if particularly adept, try and blend in with human society; however, they are required consciously to breathe and blink, both habits which would be subconsciously noted by people if absent. The vampire's skin is also naturally cool, even cold, to the touch; they can also appear cyanotic as a result of the lack of blood supply to the skin (which, as mentioned above, is usually pale, even translucent). All these visual and tactile cues can give the hunting Strigoi away.

The principal methods of Strigoi dispatch are the complete immolation of the Strigoi's body, dismemberment and decapitation, and finally staking through the heart. For creating a stake, hawthorn is the most popular wood, probably for entirely superstitious reasons; otherwise iron or silver work best. These two metals seem to react toxically with vampire blood. A scientific reason may lie in the iron ion that forms the heme group in haemoglobin. Vampire blood in types such as the Strigoi has undergone mutations, probably as a result of the vampire vector and its mutagens, and the catastrophic addition of iron or silver into the Strigoi's body may trigger a cascade effect or cytokine storm, a massive overreaction of the vampire's immune system.

Sunlight or ultraviolet light are also potent weapons against Strigoi, as light sensitivity is seen in extremis as porphyria in the Strigoi, where it can cause blistering, scarring and vomiting, and ultimately destruction.

Finally, some Strigoi are vulnerable to amuletic attack. This is most common amongst the older vampires, who shy away from and can even be harmed by the touch of religious weaponry and icons, such as crosses and holy water. Researchers have yet to ascertain why this would be so, but it is generally thought that centuries of psychosomatic belief have rendered the older Strigoi physically vulnerable to such methods as blessed stones or incense pushed into the orifices of the vampire's body, crosses of garlic or holy water placed on the sleeping vampire, or fumigating the grave.

These methods are not to be relied on in combat; the surest way to destroy a Strigoi is to use the first four methods. However, SAU units retain strong superstitious and theological beliefs, and all their weapons and ammunition are blessed and consecrated.

Like most depictions of non-haemophagic male vampires, this drawing shows a demonic creature tormenting his victim. In reality, these creatures appear as very handsome humans and most of their victims are willing participants. (PD)

Non-Haemophagic Vampires

European non-haemophagic vampires (non-blood drinkers) feed off of heat and energy. These are harvested by the vampire. This method of feeding also seems to provide as opportunity for the male and female vampire to procreate.

The male vampire is more demonic than vampiric. Visually and behaviorally, they are both largely indistinguishable from humans. The demonic portrayals of them are usually dream representations and do not reflect their usually very handsome outward appearance. Their methods of seduction may be pheromonal but may also be simple attraction. The victims are not exsanguinated, but drained of energy. Some succumb to exhaustion as a result of these attacks, although the term "attack" may be misleading, as many victims willingly participate and can even become addicted.

The the non-haemophagic female vampire seduces males for their energy and "seed." The attacks can take place over a considerable period, weeks, even months, and can be brutal.

The generally beautiful vampire may exhibit animalistic features such as bird-like feet or a reptilian tail, perhaps as a result of the loss of control. As with the non-haemophagic male vampire, many victims exhibit exhaustion but are willing, if confused, quarries. Death can be through nervous exhaustion, shock or heart failure; as such, many deaths can be hidden as natural causes. Victims can only be determined via long-term assessment.

Vulnerabilities and Termination

The male and female non-haemophagic vampires vary in their reaction to religious symbols and icons; it may be largely down to the individual and its upbringing. Many have been found to be immune to amuletic attack, and then it is a matter of conventional means (fire, dismemberment/decapitation, staking, sunlight or UV light).

Hybrid Offspring

The the offspring of the non-haemophagic vampire are known as a cambion. Initially they are believed to be stillborn, as they have no heartbeat or pulse at birth. However, at around the age of seven, the cambion manifests itself into an apparently human child. Before then, it relies on the overpowering maternal instinct of the mother to keep it "alive." Cuckolding the mother like this is often done at the expense of other children, who may end up as the cambion's first victims.

DHAMPIR HUNTERS

The best-known type of human/vampire hybrid is the Dhampir (Dhampiresa is the female), usually the result of a coupling between a human female and a Mullo. They are largely beholden to genetics as to which traits are dominant, but they form roughly two divisions. Division 1 consists of long-lived "immortals" with photophobia and zoomutation, but are non-haemophagic. Division 2 defines short-lived "humans" with exaggerated features, dark hair and pronounced canines. They can eat normal food but are generally haemophagic, which provides strength and speed but makes them hyper-metabolic. This might explain their short lives; they literally burn out.

Dhampirs of both sexes are often the most effective vampire hunters, something that has become a tradition dating back centuries. Types from both divisions have joined European SAUs, and with their heightened senses and physical abilities, have proved skilled trackers and hunters, the result of which is that they are particularly hated by the Strigoi and their kin.

These Dhampir are often tragic figures. Vampires will hunt and kill anyone remotely related to them by blood or friendship, resulting in some of the worst atrocities carried out by the Strigoi. As such, they usually choose to live lonely lives, without families or romantic relationships. However, the formation of the SAUs did give the Dhampirs hope of forming close bonds within the units, not unlike those seen amongst elite Special Forces formations.

This drawing of an attack is probably a somewhat accurate depiction. (Mary Evans)

However, as it does not rely on milk, the father or a suitable "nanny" can raise it. On maturing, the resulting children are often beautiful, very intelligent and extremely manipulative. They lack empathy and display psychotic traits but also know how to confuse and obfuscate their true natures; they will eat normal food, but are often bulimic. They are also provocative, especially as the males develop into adults.

UNESCO studies into vampire evolution indicate that the non-haemophagic vampires could represent an ancestral form of vampire. However, the cambions (the offspring of the non-haemophagic vampires) appear to be the first "true" European vampires, with previously inert traits such as zoomutation and haemophagy activated.

Chapter 3 - North American Vampires

North America as a whole seems to have been largely free of vampirism until the arrival of Europeans. Humans have been in North America for 12,000 years or more and the indigenous population has developed a rich mythology, yet there is little that could be interpreted as pertaining to vampires. Various tribes do tell of "mosquito men," a humanoid version of the insect that stealthily sucks out the brains of its victims through a proboscis, but there seems to be no truth to the legends. Another possibility is the Wendigo (sometimes written as Windigo). Most closely associated with the Algonquin Indian peoples of North America's northeastern coastline and forests, it is said to be a monster transformed from human form, or a spirit possessing a human host. Its transformation is said to be the result of the sin of consuming human flesh. In fact it seems to be an Indian parable against the dangers of cannibalism, and several Native American nations have variations of the Wendigo, including the Ojibwa, Cree, Innu, Abenake and Micmac.

While some claim the Wendigo were giants, many descriptions of the monster do seem strikingly familiar to the vampire hunter: they are said to be skeletally emaciated with deathly pale and decayed-looking skin, cold, dead hearts but bright eyes, and to be insatiably greedy for flesh.

Still, taken as a whole, it is clear that Indian mythology is far more redolent with warnings against the dangers of cannibalism than the threat of vampirism. It does indeed seem that the true vampires arrived in North America with European colonists.

Armageddon Time

The notion of Satan abroad upon the face of the earth had been preached since the 15th century in Europe and led to the generally held belief that supernatural evil was ever-present and part and parcel of daily life. With plague and war epidemic across the continent, there was also a mounting sense of impending Armageddon in both a very literal and also a theological sense.

One of the results of this growing apocalyptic terror was the fueling of religious hysteria, triggering waves of persecution. The vampires of Europe were also obvious targets and, despite their physical prowess, fell victim to blood-soaked pogroms. Not only were they justifiably blamed for being inherently evil, as well as child stealers and seducers of maidens, but also as the less justifiable cause of crop failures, pandemics and political intrigue.

Of course, religious persecution extended far and wide, and when Puritan Europeans were victimized, they sometimes took charters across the Atlantic to the wide-open spaces of the North American Eden. Naturally, vampires secreted themselves amongst them (there are no records of how many) to escape the stakes, fires and crosses.

Evidence is sparse and most of what we know from the time is largely the result of speculation, but it seems that it was the older, more wily and venerable Strigoi who hid in plain sight amongst the Puritans. Some non-haemophagic types may well have been amongst them, who could tolerate the sun and were resistant to amuletic attack. They could also have feigned seasickness to keep themselves hidden below decks, beyond suspicion during the long crossing, and even fed on rats if need be.

Their new homes were far from the fairytale castles and aristocratic mausoleums of Europe. They were also surrounded by dogmatic, suspicious, paranoid and belligerently pious Europeans who practiced the most extreme Calvinism, people who believed that to deny the existence of the supernatural was to deny the existence of angels and therefore of God. This was a certain way to guarantee a one-way trip to the stake.

A rather fanciful depiction of events during the Salem witch trials. The connection between the trials and vampires is still a hotly debated topic amongst academics. (PD)

As such, these vampires had to proceed with extreme caution. Inquisition investigations indicate that often vampires portrayed themselves as the most austere and frugal of zealots, eating lightly and living simple lives. They were usually single, instead claiming to devote themselves to their one true love, the worship of God. Ironically they were often seen as the most virtuous of the colonists.

While it was dangerous to feed within such confined and familiar quarters, there was a ready supply of victims awaiting their arrival in the form of the indigenous population. And if things went wrong, they could kill their Puritan hosts and blame it on the local Indians.

The power struggles between English, French and Dutch settlers, and the various Native American nations on the Atlantic coast, resulted in massacres and atrocities by all sides. This was a "happy time" for the vampires, who could move freely, often acting as scouts, trappers or hunters, while killing at will, with little suspicion falling on them or concern about the likelihood of supernatural agents at work. They could also begin "turning" individuals and building their numbers.

The Crucible

There are no records of vampires being killed during this tumultuous period; equally there are no conclusive victims of haemophagy. However, alleged witches were being executed as early as 1647. Minister Cotton Mathers wrote, in his 1689 book on witchcraft, of children being possessed by spells around what was to become the evil eye of the witchcraft maelstrom: Salem, Massachusetts.

Much of the carnage that followed seems to have been nothing more than mass hysteria stoked by the settling of old family scores. In such a tinderbox environment, it only took a disgruntled neighbor accusing the wife of another for the fuse to be lit. And in such a pious atmosphere, the men whose duty it was to uphold the scrupulous morality of the colonies could not ignore accusations of supernatural devilry.

As such, whether the first cases were secular malice hidden beneath religious zeal or not, it touched off an inferno. By the end of 1692, 20 people were dead, mainly women, executed for various witchcraft-related crimes.

Whilst historically interesting, the Salem witch trials would seem to have little bearing on the matter at hand, were it not for one factor: all the initial victims of the supposed witchcraft were young women, as young as nine and as old as 12. Their hysteria has been attributed to anything from pathological fear of Indian attack to ergot poisoning. However, many of these girls would have been entering puberty and would have been easy prey for a stealthy non-haemophagic male vampire. The evidence is entirely circumstantial, but remains a curious footnote in the development of vampirism in North America.

The Gilded Age

As the European settlers expanded in number and slowly started pushing west, on the American eastern seaboard new hunting grounds were springing up for the vampires and non-haemophagic predators. Early cities such as New York, Chicago, Washington and Philadelphia contained sprawling slums lacking the most basic law enforcement and rife with crime. Murder and death by illness were everyday occurrences and an experienced and stealthy vampire could easily find prey.

Again, there is little in the way of all but the most circumstantial of evidence to track the activities of vampires. However, Vatican records show vampire hunters were dispatched to the New World in the early 19th century to follow up on the witch-hunting hysteria, but also to look into a number of unusual deaths reported by trappers in and around Minnesota that were attributed to wolf attack. While wolves maintained a dreadfully savage reputation until well into the 20th century, Vatican vampire hunters were wily and astute enough to know wolves rarely, if ever, killed humans. More to the point, the attacks were of such notable violence that reports of them made their way across the Atlantic and into the hands of the Inquisition. However, the hunters were unable to ascertain the true nature of the attacks and further exploration of the region by the inquisitors found no evidence to support the presence of vampires.

Unlike Bram Stoker's *Dracula*, the 1872 vampire novel, *Carmilla*, by Joseph Sheridan Le Fanu, is thought by many to be based upon real events. (PD)

Meanwhile, a new wave of immigrants began enjoying the fruits of the burgeoning United States of America. Charles Dudley Warner and Mark Twain coined the term "the Gilded Age" to describe, in barbed satire, the chronic polarizing of American society. While most American citizens scratched out a living below the poverty line, an elite hierarchy were embracing the sociological thinking of British philosopher Herbert Spencer. It was he who coined the term "survival of the fittest" while describing Darwin's treatise on evolution, *On the Origin of Species*. His social Darwinism was seized upon by a new generation of steel magnates and business entrepreneurs who took a very literal view of the theory of evolution in industrial terms. They set

Another drawing from *Carmilla*, the first story to note that even female vampires seem generally more interested in female victims. (PD)

about using Spencer's philosophy to ruthlessly exploit the environment and their employees, justifying their worst excesses as proof of their "evolutionary" success.

Naturally, the Old World vampires of Europe were very much at home. A number of them, mainly those who were centuries old, had amassed considerable fortunes by the time they arrived in the US. Most were fleeing the increasingly sophisticated and organized vampire hunters and, with little experience of vampirism, Americans seemed easy prey.

Easily able to bribe their way ashore and into relative comfort, these new arrivals quickly set themselves up as rich business tycoons, investing old wealth in new industries: steel, railways, communications.

While wealth allows a certain amount of eccentricity to explain odd behavior, these New World vampires set about developing strategies to integrate into American society that remain effective even today. They began the practice of using human proxies, humans surgically modified to look like the vampire, to allow them to be seen under any circumstances, in daylight and at social functions. But, where possible, the vampires remained shadowy figures even as they fully embraced the tenants of social Darwinism. This provided not just cheap labor but ready supplies of easily disposable food.

Vampires Today

Having accumulated considerable fortunes, it is easy for the New World vampires to use money and their own innate powers to control considerable material holdings from deep in the shadows. Many vanish into highly secure underground worlds that are very difficult for the vampire hunters to

●REC
00:47:23:05

penetrate. Even identifying the vampires amongst the industrial elite requires a total change of approach, one that embraces psychology and criminology to spot tell-tale behavior patterns. Assessing for psychopathy and narcissistic personality disorders is one avenue of pursuit. Another is studying certain areas of criminality. Wily and cunning, these vampires are rarely clumsy or stupid enough to leave any overt sign of their activities behind, but to keep themselves well fed, and with plenty of money at their disposal, some have invested in human trafficking, prostitution and even slavery. Wealth has also made it very easy for them to dispose of their victims. Unlike the vampires of popular culture, they do not gather in covens of leather and silk-clad Goths drinking only the finest blood from champagne goblets, or in bordellos that cater to very specific tastes. They would never be so crass or blatant. Instead, they glide effortlessly through boardrooms and exclusive, isolated and luxurious resorts, invisible to the populace at large.

However, the rise of the Internet and global, instantly accessible communication has proved disastrous for the New World vampire. Operations by SAU in the Old World, during the breakup of Yugoslavia, showed that the mass of information being generated by news outlets and intelligence sources worldwide makes it much harder for the vampires to obscure their tracks. This has finally allowed UNESCO and the SAU to begin actively pursuing and eliminating the New World vampires who have for so long escaped eradication.

These efforts were given an unexpected boost by the terrorist attacks of September 11, 2001, and the subsequent passing of the Patriot Act the following month. This legislation allows for the indefinite detaining of suspects, the searching of homes and businesses without consent, the use of roving wiretaps, and the searching of financial, phone, library and email records without a court order.

(Opposite) The single, surviving still from *VampCam*.

VAMPCAM

In May 2009, a group of four vampire fanatics – all in their late teens – from Detroit, Michigan, decided to embark on a reality series to document vampires. Dubbed *VampCam*, this short-lived show was filmed over three consecutive weekends. The enthusiastic youngsters would go out into the night and search for vampire activity to film and upload to their website.

The youngsters successfully managed to record genuine vampire action on three occasions. Filmed at night near the downtown Detroit area, the 40- and 50-second clips showed groups of vampires engaged in feeding frenzies.

The website was taken down shortly after the third video was posted, which showed the young cameraman being mauled to death by the vampires he was filming. The FBI reportedly took the site down, pending an investigation, though no further information has ever been released. Naturally, all reference to the site has been removed and the three surviving youngsters have not been seen or heard from since. Though rumors suggest that they entered witness protection, the reality is likely to be far more sinister. All that remains of *VampCam* is a single still from the action that evening, grabbed from the site seconds before it was shut down.

Other informational areas that help in the detection of vampires include:

- Tracking missing persons: looking for patterns not just over months or years, but decades.
- Law enforcement websites: monitoring these can expose unusual murders or crimes e.g. hospital or blood bank break-ins.
- The in-depth study of fiscal records, using specially trained accountants to monitor the movement of money and to look for unusual spending patterns.

The Special Action Unit Expansion

The global "war on terror" has provided a massive cash injection for many shady and covert organizations, and some of that money has found its way to SAU. This has allowed the building of a new infrastructure that provided a serious increase in the capabilities of the organization. New interrogation facilities were built. While much of the information regarding these "black sites" remains understandably classified, it can be revealed that the holding cells are circular and built from treated stainless-steal and ceramic composites that are largely indestructible, and equipped with batteries of strong ultraviolet lamps. The SAU operators use modified bomb disposal suits, acid-etched with religious iconography and featuring embedded amulets.

SAU is also believed to have its own fleet of specially equipped aircraft used for extraordinary rendition to these facilities, which are located worldwide. It is understood these bases and aircraft have already been put to use by SAU for the interrogation of High Value Targets (HVR). The unit has also received training from the Joint Personnel Recovery Agency (JPRA), a highly classified US military program originally set up covertly to remove or rescue

A CH-47 Chinook taking part in SAU operations. (US Department of Defense)

US military personnel from "denied" areas – enemy territory. JPRA also runs a program called SERE: Survival, Evasion, Resistance, Escape. It was originally intended to prepare the likes of US fighter pilots or Special Forces teams for the eventuality of falling into enemy hands and being tortured by putting them through a grueling training program. To this end, JPRA has amassed what might be considered the definitive library on physical and psychological torture techniques. Following the 9/11 attack, the US government asked JPRA to "reverse engineer" the methods studied so they could be used against terrorist suspects. The resulting interrogation manual was adapted by SAU, aided by JPRA operatives and SERE instructors, for use against vampires, in the hope of exposing their network of fellow haemophages and also to seize their assets, the money from which was ploughed back into the SAU.

It is, however, a time-consuming process. Effective interrogation does not rely on "medieval" techniques such as beatings and stress positions, but on the intelligent use of coercive pressure that is difficult to endure. The standard techniques are in many ways redundant when dealing with vampires, especially ones as resilient as Old World vampires, but these methods can be adapted. If a vampire is found to be susceptible to amuletic attack, the use of religious icons such as crosses can be used as part of the interrogation. However, the most effective methods still remain the development of a rapport with the HVR, winning their trust through the applied use of psychological threat and more subtle physical attacks such as "cold turkey" – the removal of their food source, which has a similar effect on vampires as does the removal of drugs from an addict. These are far more effective approaches than using a magnifying glass to burn a vampire with directed sunlight; such physical abuse tends just to stiffen their resolve. As such, SAU interrogators are required to be intellectually and psychologically robust.

MISTER X

Following 9/11, the SAU decided to make use of the sudden flood of intelligence data and resources available to them to try and land their first US target, nicknamed rather sardonically as "Mister X."

The SAU seconded selected members of the FBI's infamous Behavioral Science unit and the JPRA for a long-term black op to eliminate Mister X. Using FBI undercover agents, the SAU planted a number of individuals in a human trafficking organization. Its operatives had been tracking an individual they believed was a buyer for a possible vampire with a taste for the "mother country." While sporadically acquiring a number of young women as livestock from across the globe, the number bought from Eastern Europe remained high – high enough to draw interest from SAU. An FBI agent was able to develop a relationship with the buyer, and while the latter revealed little, the agent was able to garner enough intelligence to convince SAU that their hunch had been right.

Intelligence gathering began on Mister X himself. Due to the vampire's experience and obvious intellect, this had to be very long-term and subtle. The "sting" required a great deal of time and money to be spent. Agents from the FBI and SAU were set up as executives in a number of technology and communications companies. As many of these were formed following the dot.com bonanza, the agents were able to develop solid résumés, and as the dot.com bubble waxed and waned, the agents moved freely through various boardrooms without drawing attention to themselves. These were sleeper agents in the truest sense, developing new lives that could withstand the most intensive scrutiny.

A number of agents were used in the hope that one would be able to get close enough to Mister X. This "scattergun" approach finally paid off when one of the "executives" was hired by the vampire's company. Working up through the ranks, the agent finally gained a position within X's inner circle and began gleaning the intelligence necessary to look at rendering the vampire.

(Opposite) A custom-built, SAU imprisonment and interrogation chamber. Even in such a secure facility, heavily armored suits are still required for all interactions with captured vampires.

THE PSYCHOPATH TEST

One recent addition to the SAU armory has been the Hare Psychopathy Test, developed in the 1970s to study personality traits in perceived psychopaths. The clinical markers derived from the test's questions were studied by vampire experts in the US as a possible method of identifying vampires. Such is the confusion between psychopathic, sociopathic, antisocial, narcissistic and histrionic personality disorders that singling out a vampire takes an expert eye, and SAU operatives now include a number of brilliant behavioral analysts and profilers, and forensic psychiatrists, some recruited from law enforcement agencies around the world.

In layman's terms, there are a number of markers to look for, although the differences between vampire and psychopath are subtle:

- They are charming, charismatic, confident and self-assured.
- Shrewd, sly, deceptive, manipulative, unscrupulous and dishonest.
- Lack empathy, feeling no concern for those in grief or suffering loss, although they can "play act" at being sympathetic; mimicry of other human emotional behaviors is another trait.
- While outwardly gregarious, they actually lack any warmth towards others.
- They are rarely in any kind of long-term relationship and tend to live what could be termed nomadic existences, remaining independent. Should they be capable of relationships, these tend to be very transitory. However, finding partners is easy, as they are coercive and enticing.
- Unscrupulous in exploiting an individual's or society's weak spots.
- Usually associate only with a very defined peer group, usually of similar status or role (industrialists, businessmen, etc.).
- Rarely, if ever, ill and generally have no records of injuries (US vampires have been known to fake records to throw investigators and hunters off their trail).
- Usually physically attractive but reclusive or faking a "rich and shameless" lifestyle through use of proxies or doubles.

This blurry, night-vision photograph is the best image to have reached the public from the raid that captured "Mister X." (US Department of Defense)

A JPRA/SAU team was put on standby. An aircraft was kept fueled, crewed and on 24-hour alert at a military airport close to the city where Mister X was based. The problem was that the vampire rarely left his penthouse that was actually underneath his offices, making intelligence gathering on its layout and final ingress into the building very difficult.

The capture team had a stroke of luck when the FBI agents learned the date and whereabouts of a delivery from the traffickers. In a very carefully orchestrated operation, the trucks delivering the young women were intercepted and the original victims skillfully replaced with an entirely female contingent of FBI agents, specially trained by JPRA. Using various weapons and equipment carefully secreted about their persons, they were able to affect an escape from their holding pens, timing it in late afternoon when studies had shown the vampire to be at his weakest.

At the first sign of trouble, Mister X bolted for an underground escape route that took him into a network of storm drains. Anticipating this, the capture team had the tunnels covered. Using a number of specialized weapons, the SAU and JPRA operatives were able to secure Mister X, although a number of individuals were injured or killed. Using a helicopter to take the immobilized vampire to the military airport, X was quickly airborne and taken to a "black site" in a North African country and questioned on his knowledge of other vampires. He was subsequently terminated and his assets dissolved and disbursed. A cover story alluded to Mister X's sudden death due to medical problems.

Chapter 4 - African Vampires

A Vampire by Any Other Name

The Ghanaian Asanbosam is one of several vampire species whose evolutionary paths can be traced back to the bat. Most are quick to assume that the vampire bat is the natural forefather of the Asanbosam, but its origins are, in fact, closer to home.

The vampire bat belongs to the microbat (Microchiroptera) family and is native to the regions of Central and South America – the home of the Chupacabra, whose origins are deeply rooted in evolution (see the chapter on South America). However, the Asanbosam is considered to be a subspecies of the megabat (Megachiroptera) family, which can be found among the forests of Africa. It was once thought that the micro- and megabats shared a common ancestor, but they have two very distinct evolutionary chains. Unlike the microbats, who evolved from small, shrew-like insectivores, megabats developed from something far more human: primates.

Asanbosam Spotting

At an average height of 6.5 feet (2 meters) and with incredible muscle mass, an Asanbosam strikes an impressive figure. Taller than most men, it has evolved quickly to survive in the forests of Ghana. The creature started life smaller than it appears now. As a megabat subspecies, its original diet consisted largely of fruit and nectar, but this would not have been enough to sustain the Asanbosam's physique that we see today.

Like other primates, the Asanbosam are curious animals. In an effort to supplement the paltry diet provided by the flowers and plants of the forest, they turned to other sources in their immediate vicinity. Once the vampires had sunk their teeth into the forest fauna, they quickly developed a taste for blood; a small drop was all it took to trigger a reaction in their minds, sending them into a frenzied state. The taste of blood ignited the impatient, angry and territorial behavior that had remained dormant for much of its early life.

Driven by bloodlust, the Asanbosam craved a new food supply. Such was their need to ingest blood and protein that they had no choice but to look at other ways to catch prey. They did not have to search far; the trees were teeming with wildlife, from birds to snakes, and even monkeys. The Asanbosam would eat anything they could sink their teeth into. Seeing the animals flee only fueled their salivating. They became transfixed by the "easy prey" that surrounded them, and it was during their pursuit of other food sources that the Asanbosam began to develop their hunting skills.

One of the most largely reported features of the creature is its hooked feet. Descriptions of these "hooks" vary, from large-scale fishing hooks to slightly curved human-like feet. The latter is closest to the reality. As a result of their evolution in the Ghanaian forests, the Asanbosam have developed a natural balancing ability, and they use the incredibly powerful muscles in their legs and feet to distribute their weight evenly.

Despite their imposing grandeur and gruff exterior, Asanbosam are relatively nervous on the floors of the forest, understandably so, having spent their evolution living entirely among the trees of Ghana's forests. Taking the lead from their bat kindred, the Asanbosam learned to dangle upside down from overhanging branches using their hooked feet and unparalleled balancing ability. Consequently, they are able to scoop up any prey that scuttles below. They also possess a prehensile tail, which is crucial to their balance when moving through the trees or hanging down from them. An Asanbosam can use its tail as a distraction for prey, and exercises it much like a snake charmer.

A reconstruction of an Asanbosam made from a partially dismembered corpse recovered in 2007. (Reconstruction by Hauke Kock)

An Asanbosam's body is lean and incredibly toned, and the musculature of the creature is a sight to behold. Suspended upside down, an Asanbosam would need to be able to use its core stability to maintain its static and composed posture. They are able to stretch their long, lithe bodies, so that even from a great height they can reach smaller animals passing below, and use their incredible upper-body strength to drag prey into the trees to be eaten.

The Asanbosam use their prehensile feet as hands. Should the situation call for it, the creature can reverse its position and hang from trees using its hands, thereby leaving its feet free to grab prey from underneath. The Asanbosam's dark skin tone allows them to remain camouflaged in their surroundings, and keen eyesight ensures that they can peer through the dense, dark forests by day or by night.

Having evolved into vicious hunters, the Asanbosam use their claws and teeth to tear into their prey, ripping open the skin and shredding through muscle, bone and cartilage. In true, classic vampire style, they tend to aim for the neck first to ensure a quick death. Oral stories have described the vampire's teeth and claws as resembling iron, but there is nothing in the physiology or evolution of the Asanbosam that would indicate the presence of such a material.

The flying fox, a subspecies of the mega bat, is the largest bat in the world and a likely candidate for being the ancestor of the Asanbosam. (PD)

Over time, the Asanbosam moved to target larger mammals that would scurry through the forest, oblivious to the fate that awaited them. Animals such as buffalo, red river hogs and the yellow-backed duiker were popular choices. But still, the hunger of the Asanbosam was not satisfied, and in the 16th century hunters returning from the forests began to tell stories of forest elephants mauled to death by unknown, evil forest spirits. Was this a sign that the vampires had begun to venture onto the forest floor? After all, it would be extremely cumbersome to drag a 6-ton elephant into the forest trees. So what caused the Asanbosam to make this giant leap?

Territory Wars

Between AD 1000 and 1400, the earliest towns built by the Akans (an ethnic group native to Ghana and consisting of several tribes) began to emerge. Their villages that populated the region were becoming bigger and brought more people into contact with the forests. Before this "urbanization," human-Asanbosam encounters had been rare, as the Asanbosam lived deep enough in the forests to avoid discovery by the Akans. But with the population gradually building, the Akans needed to go further into the forests to find the food they needed to provide for their people. As a result, Asanbosam sightings became more frequent, and the mythology of the creature was introduced into the oral traditions of the Akan people.

Deforestation in Ghana had been a problem as far back as 450 BC, when the ancient Greek historian Herodotus documented losses of forest resources in sub-Saharan Africa. During the late 15th and 16th centuries AD, when Europeans arrived in the country, the economy of Ghana shifted from one that relied primarily on hunting and gathering to one that focused on agricultural produce. The traders imported crops that would adapt easily to forest conditions, such as bananas, sorghum, and cassava from southeast Asia and the New World.

As farming expanded, the population of Ghana increased significantly, encouraging numbers of Akans to migrate across the country's forests in the search for good farmland. This land was not easy to come by, leading to a significant clearing of forest vegetation that has continued to this day. To put this into perspective: at one point, around two-thirds of Ghana was covered with tropical forest. Today, that stands at approximately 25 percent.

Stories of Asanbosam attacks were quick to arrive in the 16th century and became more prevalent in the following years. As forests were cut back to allow for expansion of farming, the Asanbosam habitat grew smaller. Threatened by the invasion, the creatures' primal instinct was to attack.

The Akans were not as easy to kill as the helpless antelope; they were seasoned hunters. Formed of tribes of skilled warriors, the Akans had some degree of fighting techniques. Sadly, their skills were not enough to completely overcome the Asanbosam. The might and power of the creatures were almost

Ashanti war drums, which were also historically used as part of sacrifices to the Asanbosam. (Mary Evans)

impossible to conquer, even for the Akan hunters. Survivors of Asanbosam encounters were uncommon, and as the legends took on a life of their own, it was dificult for anyone to distinguish between what was fact and what was fiction.

The Ashanti

Angry, threatened and starved, the Asanbosam took desperate measures. After millennia spent in the trees, they had no choice but to be more active in their efforts to pursue their prey, human and animal alike. Following in the footsteps of their primate forefathers, the Asanbosam mimicked the actions they witnessed; they took their cues from the Akans, recognizing similarities in the appearance and behavior. Driven by their human brothers to evolve their hunting practices, the Asanbosam literally hit the ground running.

The Ashanti, one of the tribes of the Akan, were the first tribe of people to react against the attacks of the Asanbosam in an organized way. As part of a rapid and massive expansion of the Ashanti kingdom that began in the 1670s, tribal chiefs decided that they had to act in order to combat the growing Asanbosam problem. Meeting at a clandestine location in the city of Kumasi, the capital of the Ashanti Empire, several prominent chiefs from different districts decided that hunters should be trained to specifically combat the Asanbosam.

The Ashanti are famous for being a warlike people. With their armies numbering anywhere between 200,000 and 500,000, they went on to overcome neighboring states ruled by the Denkyira, Wassa, Fante and Bono people from the mid-18th to the late 19th centuries. They even held their own against the British Empire on four occasions during the Anglo-Ashanti wars. The Ashanti region ultimately became one of the most powerful states in the central forest zones.

The Ashanti people follow the line of matrilineal descent: a mother's clan is seen as more important than the father's, with offspring inheriting a mother's flesh and blood (*mogya*) and the property and/or titles that come with her side of the family. From their father's side, a child inherits the soul or spirit (*okra*).

Consequently, potential hunters were chosen based on their genealogy, looking specifically at the physicality of the women and the character and personality of the men. Chiefs would have to scrutinize hundreds of potential fighters before they found someone suitable.

Once a prospective vampire hunter was selected, the individual would begin their training. The Ashanti had very little information to go on at this point, and so they had to prepare for any situation. After examining the many oral stories surrounding the Asanbosam, the chiefs understood that their unit would have to be trained to skillfully navigate the branches of the forests to give the hunters any chance at slaying a vampire.

The hunters took to the bush with ease – after all, their ancestors had lived as forest dwellers. They would train on the forest outskirts, bare-footed to grip the branches that they ran along, and working to improve their balance. Nutrition was also important, and vampire hunters made their bodies as lean as possible to minimize their weight. It was important to seize any opportunity to eliminate an Asanbosam in the maze of trees and branches. If a branch snapped under the weight of a hunter, not only would he lose his opening, but probably his life.

The hunters became skilled in the use of a number of different weapons. Many would already be trained in the use of short spears and a small knife. These were no ordinary weapons: both were tipped with gold, a metal that the Ashanti held in high regard and an element for which the region would become famous. The weapons were light and small in order to minimize weight and allow for a greater ease of movement in the cramped forest conditions.

As the hunters became more advanced, they learned to wield the *hunga munga*, a weapon resembling a cross between a knife and a hatchet. This lightweight weapon had a series of straight and curved blades, and its composition meant that the blade would make contact with its target at any angle when thrown.

(Opposite) Many Asanbosam hunters have discovered that the best way to find the creature is to follow its prey.

ASANBOSAM WORSHIP

Not all chiefs believed in killing Asanbosam. Some worshiped the creatures, believing that the Asanbosam would prevent those who deified them from coming to harm. These chiefs, protected by their bodyguards (*abrafor*), would hold rituals that involved moving in rhythmic fashion to the beat of giant drums adorned with human skulls as a mark of sacrifice to the Asanbosam. The *abrafor* would behead their brethren in ritualistic practices to appease the gods, and the more skulls there were on a drum, the more powerful the chiefs were believed to be. Further sacrificial rites included the use of blood in certain celebrations.

Every weapon, accessory and item of clothing was chosen with the greatest precision. The Ashanti chiefs thought it essential that hunters were decorated with powerfully enchanted totems to protect them against the supernatural Asanbosam. In the face of the unknown, the chiefs turned to witch doctors and the mystical powers of magic, or *juju*, to help the hunters in their crusade against the vampires. This was dangerous territory, with the spiritual customs as dark and mysterious as the perception of the Asanbosam.

The most common crafters of *juju* were a cult of Muslim holy men called marabouts, who traveled around Africa, dazzling the people of the continent with their magic. The chiefs sought out good *juju* to combat the evil *juju* of the Asanbosam. But there was more to this magic than verbal enchantments. Marabouts were asked to provide the strongest totems possible, and hunters would carry skulls and bones imbued with magical properties on a ring of string, a sort of charm bracelet, which would offer protection against the Asanbosam.

One of the most important artifacts, or fetishes, was a silver ring given to each hunter to wear. Within these rings was a text bearing unknown scripture provided by the marabouts. Over time, these rings were passed down from hunter to hunter, and they took on a mythical and superstitious quality that eventually made it taboo to try and read the scripture.

Chiefs appealed to the best herbalist healers (*odunsini*) in the villages to provide medical care and teach the hunters how to use the plants and flowers scattered throughout the forest to heal their wounds. Each village also had an *okomfo* (a fetish priest or white wizard) who would become possessed by deities and channel the godly power to help fight the evil lurking inside Ghana's rainforests.

There was little in the way of clothing. Hunters wore traditional African war cloth, *batakari*, in colors that would help them blend into their surroundings. There were also hints of red, yellow and orange. The hunters were surrounded by death, and they believed that warm colors that represented fire – a symbol of rebirth and life – would help to protect the hunters from the evil they were facing.

Once training was over, and the chiefs felt they had done all they could, the hunters entered the forest. From that point, they were on their own.

Asanbosam have evolved into vicious killers with powerful jaws, easily capable of tearing off a man's arm. (Reconstruction by Hauke Kock)

The First Hunt

The vampire hunters quickly learned that the Asanbosam were nothing like they had ever faced before. Unlike the other, more supernatural vampires that we have come to know, the Asanbosam were relatively easy to maim and kill, providing the hunters could get close enough. Unluckily for the hunters, by the time the Ashanti had sent their first organized unit into the forests, the vampires were literally foaming at their mouths; they would twitch at any sound, smell or sight that could potentially lead to their next meal. A lot of blood was shed during those first raids, and the trained Ashanti vampire hunters suffered heavy losses.

Despite these early, unsuccessful raids, each new hunter-Asanbosam encounter yielded at least some slight fragment of information on the vampires. The hunters recognized that the Asanbosam were acutely aware of their surroundings. The branches, twigs and leaves of the trees acted like the threads of a spider's web, with the vampires able to detect the slightest hint of movement. However, they were easily distracted by their food, too absorbed by the meal wandering across their path.

Physical balance was such an essential part of the behavior of the Asanbosam that the hunters quickly learned to incapacitate their targets by severing the tail. Close-range attacks were rarely successful. Any hunter that survived a melee with one of the creatures did so out of luck more than skill, particularly if a fight broke out in the trees. Knocking the vampires to the ground earned the hunters an advantage; though the Asanbosam had begun to venture onto the forest floors, they had not developed the confidence that matched their abilities in the trees, which hindered their fighting skills.

Yet the hunters found more than they bargained for during their patrols of the Ghanaian forests. They discovered that the Asanbosam were perhaps not the malicious vampires that they had been portrayed as. Though their loss of habitat fueled their violent and extreme behavior, there was a more malevolent presence pulling at the strings. Another vampire was sweeping across the country, enacting terrible and deadly deeds upon innocent Ashanti.

A *hunga munga* throwing knife. Just one of the many odd weapons developed in Africa and adapted to hunting the Asanbosam. (Brooklyn Museum)

Toil and Trouble

Obayifo are a powerful and parasitic species, and like the Asanbosam, they are not considered to be a "conventional" vampire. "Obayifo" is the name given to a person who has two spirits – one neutral, the other evil – residing within them. The vampire fights an eternal inner struggle to keep the malevolent spirit from overcoming their mind and soul. Should an Obayifo become overpowered by the evil spirit, the darker side of its personality emerges with the ability to wield incredible magic. Though their behavior and appearance is similar to the Western idea of a witch – for example, they gather round pots known as *kukuo* to create powerful elixirs using the blood of their victims – they are officially classed as vampires.

An Obayifo can go undetected for years, as they integrate themselves into communities without being noticed. Pro-vampire sociologists and historians believe they do so to protect the villages they inhabit from evil spirits, as a sort of *okomfo*.

Their control over the magical arts led some to believe that they were good magicians gone mad with power. Some of the blame was placed at the feet of the marabouts, leading to a number of innocent men being falsely accused and succumbing to a violent death. Others thought that the Obayifo were responsible for summoning the Asanbosam, who were considered to be dark spirits, to scare away European colonists in an effort to protect the land and the forests. They were half-right.

Ashanti Priests performing an unknown blood ceremony. (Mary Evans)

Obayifo are protectors of the land. The spirits within them are aligned to the flow of energy that runs through the earth itself. With Ghana under threat of deforestation, the Obayifo sought to rid the region of its offenders. Recognizing the susceptibility of the Asanbosam mind in its blood-frenzied state, the Obayifo were able to manipulate the forest vampires into doing their bidding.

There are two ways to identify an Obayifo. The first is by their "shifty eyes" (rapid eye movement, or saccades), a result of their anxiety at being discovered at any time as their eyes shift to survey the area. Secondly, Obayifo have an obsession with food, particularly red meat, and they can be spotted prowling around when a meal is being cooked. They are desperate to feed, and they turn into ravenous animals in the presence of food, not unlike their forest friends, the Asanbosam.

While Obayifo are vampires in the strictest sense, they depend on other sources of food to satisfy their hunger. As empathic vampires, they use their psychic ability to feed off the telepathic waves of pain and misery that radiate from the organisms that surround them. They have a particular taste for children; the innocent nature gives a child's blood and psychic vibrations a refined and untainted quality. A child's melancholy is like nectar to the Obayifo; they are so utterly intoxicated by the purity of their essence.

One unexplainable revelation about the Obayifo is its ability to transform into a ball of light in order to possess humans and animals. It is very easy to tell when a possession has occurred, as light emanates from a number of areas, including the armpits and anus. This method of possession has baffled the scientific and paranormal communities. It is only employed by the Obayifo in extreme circumstances, often in times of crisis, using a host body to escape when the vampire has been discovered. Perhaps, in their urgency, an Obayifo cannot focus its energy and is therefore unable to keep its power under control.

There is no known way to exorcise the vampire from its victims. One must simply wait until the Obayifo is finished with the possession. Unfortunately, most victims don't survive the experience, not because of the Obayifo itself, but because the victim is normally killed by panicked villagers who are unsure how to act when greeted with such a strange and mysterious sight.

SASANBOSAM: THE TOURIST TRAP

Ghana is littered with caves. Today, most function as tourist attractions, but not all are as empty as they seem.

During their evolution, the Asanbosam line divided, creating an offshoot vampire subspecies: the Sasanbosam. In an evolutionary path not too dissimilar from the bat, a genetic mutation led to the Sasanbosam's large fingers to extend further to create a giant hand. Living in the uppermost canopies of the rainforests, the Sasanbosam would jump from branch to branch, using the high launching points to take off. A thin membrane of skin developed between their digits, creating wings that would eventually reach a space of up to 20 feet (6 meters).

When competition for food in the forests increased, the Sasanbosam took to the skies and flew to the caves, finding solace in the dark grottos. The Sasanbosam shares many of the same traits as its Asanbosam cousins, including a taste for blood, a tail, "hooked" feet, and an aversion to moving along the floor. As a result, they use their feet to grip onto cave ceilings and hang down.

Tourists should beware when entering a cave. Though many caverns are reportedly uninhabited and attacks are infrequent, you can never be too sure of what is hanging overhead. The Sasanbosam is not afraid to swoop into a cave under the cover of darkness and await a meal, particularly if it knows that meal will wander in so unwittingly.

Obayifo cannot stay in these orb forms for long. If they are unable to find a host, or if they have not fed, they will enter crop fields and suck out sap and vital juices. Their ability to survive using a number of different food sources, coupled with their ultimate escape tactic, indicates that Obayifo deaths are extremely rare.

Obayifo are able to reverse their empathic feeding ability and use their power to bewitch the mind and ensnare the senses of those easily susceptible to control. One such target was the Asanbosam, whose primitive minds are easily manipulated. The Obayifo use a process that is similar to the glamor technique employed by certain other vampire types. If an Obayifo is powerful enough, they are able to control three or four Asanbosam at once, though this amount of control will weaken the Obayifo.

This ability to effectively control minds allows the Obayifo to manipulate the Asanbosam into terrorizing communities, inciting pain and misery, thereby providing the Obayifo with a greater source of nourishment. Though the vampire hunters had adapted quickly to hunting Asanbosam, the Obayifo presented an altogether different challenge.

Magic Moments

Although the Ashanti vampire hunters possessed a certain degree of *juju* knowhow, and they were adorned with enchanted items for extra protection, their skills lay in physical attack. The "magic" they wielded was simply not strong enough to combat the power of the Obayifo. In response to the new threat, the chiefs appealed to the village *okomfo* again, who recognized that it would take a formidable force to overpower the dark magic of the Obayifo.

After conversing with the gods, the *okomfo* discovered that only the combined power of the religious spirit would dispel an Obayifo. Villages consisted of close communities, and the Ashanti treated neighbors and friends as family. The *okomfo* believed that the support of this cohesive unit – trusting, respectful, selfless, and enriched with religious traditions – would infuse them with enough power to defeat the antagonistic magic of the Obayifo.

Fearful that the Obayifo would seek means of escape through possession once confronted, the *okomfo* advised the villagers on spells and charms that could be used to seal their homes. Uncooked meat was used to draw out the Obayifo, like a dog. It was placed at the entrance to the village in an attempt to draw the Obayifo as far away as possible from the living creatures it could possess.

Once distracted, it was essential to kill the Obayifo as quickly as possible. The hunters tried first to cut off the head, but were met with disastrous consequences. The blood of the Obayifo was contaminated and burned the skin of whomever it touched. When it seeped into the ground below, the surrounding land would grow infertile, and crops withered and wilted, leaving a desert-like wasteland in its place.

To avoid blood being shed, it was necessary to strangle or drown an Obayifo. With water in short supply and not wanting to contaminate the water that the villagers had access to, strangulation became the most popular method. It would require a team of hunters protected by the most powerful charms to take down an Obayifo before it was able to use its powerful magic to escape.

Ashanti vampire hunters have been protecting the nation of Ghana from Asanbosam, Obayifo, and other so-called "supernatural" creatures for more than 500 years. Thanks to their efforts, Asanbosam attacks have fallen dramatically, particularly since the beginning of the 20th century, helped by the deforestation from which the country has suffered.

Obayifo appearances have decreased, but this could simply be a result of them becoming more skilled at integrating themselves into Ghana's communities. Sightings of traveling Obayifo have been reported in Togo, Benin and Nigeria, and these countries have employed their own vampire-hunting units to tackle the threat.

At the current rate of deforestation, Ghana could lose all its forests by 2040. As the Asanbosam's habitat continues to vanish, its numbers are decreasing. Packed into such a small space, the vampires are becoming easier to take down, especially with hundreds of years of hunting experience against them. Recent findings of dead Asanbosam also show long claw marks and giant bites on their bodies. Perhaps we are witnessing a species turning on its kind in order to survive, or the rise of a new, stronger, more savage vampire species, claiming Ghana's forests for its own.

It has been recently posited that Asanbosam are simply misunderstood creatures who reacted to the loss of their habitat. After all, they peacefully coexisted with humans until rates of deforestation hit high levels. And what of the Obayifo's role as puppet master? We may never truly know if the Asansbosam's actions were their own, or the result of outside interference.

An Ashanti Juju Man. These magicians have played a large role in supplying weapons and magic to fight against both Asanbosam and Obayifo. (Mary Evans)

[1] The Kingdom of Ashanti, the Gold Coast and British Togoland adopted the legal name of "Ghana" when the country became independent on March 6, 1957. Though the country's borders and names have changed throughout the course of history, we will continue to refer to it as Ghana for the sake of simplicity.

Chapter 5 - Asian Vampires

Hopping Mad

The Jiangshi (pronounced "chong-shee") is the most notorious of the vampires in Asia, though certainly not for reasons you might expect. Its body is stiff with rigor mortis, forcing it to move around by hopping, arms outstretched like a zombie as it struggles to keep its balance.[1] The sight of one of these creatures, dressed in Qing (pronounced "ching") dynasty-style robes and with a vacant-like expression, would not leave its victim cowering in fear but doubled up with laughter.

"Jiangshi" translates as "*stiff corpse*," a term that has only helped to blur the classification of this creature. Certain members of the vampire community are loath to acknowledge that the Jiangshi is a vampire, preferring instead to categorize it as a zombie, and it is easy to see why. The process of creating a Jiangshi is not so far removed from the process of creating a zombie. Moreover, its bumbling, stumbling movements, lack of self-awareness, and apparent disinterest in anything other than food, have done much to fuel the perception that there really isn't much more to them. But like all good vampires, the threat runs much deeper.

The earliest stories of Jiangshi can be found in literature from the Qing Dynasty, which ruled imperial China from 1644–1912. There were two seminal texts from the era. The first, *Zi Bu Yu*, was a collection of true supernatural stories from writer Yuan Mei, and contained 30 Jiangshi narratives from the period. The second came from writer Ji Xiaolan, who presented teachings on Jiangshi folklore in his book *Yuewei Caotang Biji*. The two texts established the groundwork for what the vampire hunters used to train and focus their skills in order to combat the Jiangshi threat. Having an almost biblical status among the students of Asian vampires, the information provided in the two texts has not altered much from what we know today.

Spiritual Metamorphosis

The Qing-style Jiangshi is a relatively new breed of vampire, with sightings of the current iteration springing up around China during the 1970s. Throughout the Qing period, Jiangshi-sighting testimonials describe the vampires clothed in attire from the previous ruling dynasty, the Ming Dynasty (1368–1644). The Jiangshi's appearance is indicative of the length of time it takes for the conversion from human to vampire to complete, a prolonged metamorphosis that is heavily steeped in spiritualism.

Xiaolan and Mei had opposing views on the transformation of human to Jiangshi. Xiaolan alludes to chance and accident, such as the sound of thunder shocking a Jiangshi awake, or the excitement of perceiving a living person's yang rousing the vampire from its slumber. Mei's spiritualist theories are much closer to modern thought. It is now accepted that Jiangshi are created as a result of a particularly violent death, such as suicide, hanging, or drowning, or, more commonly, an improper burial. China has a strong tradition of honoring the dead, particularly with regards to one's native homeland and familial ties.

Despite looking more like a zombie than a traditional vampire, the Jiangshi are dangerous, empathic vampires. (Reconstruction by Hauke Kock)

The time taken for a human corpse to fully convert into a Jiangshi varies, though 100 years is deemed to be the minimum. However, the long process ensures that the vampire is given the best defense possible, thereby making it near impossible to destroy and one of nature's most effective killing machines.

The stimulus for creating a Jiangshi is steeped in Taoist philosophical beliefs and involves the polarity of two forces: light and dark, yin and yang, or, in this case, the *hun* and *po*. According to Taoist teachings, every living human is believed to possess a number of souls that remain balanced and harmonious: three *hun* and seven *po*. *Hun* are superior souls that appear at the moment of birth. They are the yang of a person, representing the life force or *qi* (pronounced "chi"), and as such, they are rational and virtuous. *Po* are inferior souls that come into being at conception of a human life. They embody a person's yin, the primal instincts and animalistic nature, encouraging man to covet material possessions and inciting aggression. In death, while the *hun* depart for heaven, the *po* stay within the body.

If a deceased body does not receive the proper burial rites, the *po* will initiate the Jiangshi transformation process once the *hun* have departed. Normally, "feeding" the body using sacrificial offerings that form part of the veneration of the dead would preserve the corpse and keep the *po* in their rightful place. If this practice is not observed, the corpse would eventually become consumed by the *po*, which would animate it and command the body to leave the grave and wreak havoc.

Jiangshi have been known to return to their familial home in search of their loved ones, having never been laid to rest in the proper way. This rarely ends well. Given the length of time it takes for the transformation process, the inhabitants of the home are either several generations along or unrelated to the vampire standing on their doorstep.

Surviving witnesses claim to have seen Jiangshi sucking the blood out of their victims, but this is certainly not the case. Western entertainment depicting the traditional European, bloodsucking vampire has flooded the Chinese market, influencing the perception of vampires. While it may be true that a Jiangshi encounter could result in some bloodshed, the vampire is not a haemophage. Like the African Obayifo, it is a type of psychic vampire, and instead targets a prey's *qi* using empathic abilities.

In traditional Chinese culture, it is believed that a person's *qi* sustains them, providing life and vitality. Roaming the earth as undead creatures caught between the mortal realm and the next life, Jiangshi devour *qi* in order to anchor their souls to our living realm. It is thought that with enough *qi*, a Jiangshi will be able to revert to its human state, though a successful reversal has yet to be recorded.

Jiangshi are almost blind, relying instead on their other senses to track down their victims. They are able to detect and track prey by the energy fluctuations that are caused by human breathing. The vampire's limited movement means it depends on close-range techniques to incapacitate its prey. It uses its breath as a weapon, expeling a putrid, rancid, green musk that disorients and paralyzes the target. With the unlucky victim lying in its arms, Jiangshi use a "death kiss" to suck the *qi* out, leaving their target devoid of any life force and rendering them a corpse.

The stiffness of a Jiangshi will lessen the longer they are out of the grave, allowing them to have a greater degree of flexibility and control over their limbs, which will have horrific results on a victim. If a Jiangshi feels threatened or that it has exhausted all other methods of subduing its prey, it will not hesitate to tear its target limb from limb.

Bluntly put, for the untrained, the key to escaping from a Jiangshi is not to get caught in the first place. Once trapped in its vice-like grip, or knocked out by the potent stench of its breath, it is unlikely you will live to tell the tale.

Jiangshi Journeys

The earliest surviving documentation on Jiangshi is recorded within Xiaolan's and Mei's texts from the 18th century. Much of the literature on Eastern vampires is believed to have been destroyed when the Shaolin Monastery that housed them was lit on fire by the warlord Shi Yousan in 1928. The fire raged for 40 days, destroying the temple and countless other sacred texts and martial arts manuals, some of which were centuries old. All that remained were wall frescoes painted with images of fighting monks, and stone tablets that stated, somewhat ironically, that the destruction of the temple was prohibited.

The role of the Shaolin Monastery, built in AD 495–496 and nestled among the Songshan mountain range in Zhengzhou, Henan Province, and its eponymous monks runs much deeper than simply being a library for old vampiric texts. The Jiangshi have a long history with the Shaolin monks, who helped in the transportation of Jiangshi bodies.

The appropriate and honorable burial of a deceased family member held great importance to the people of China. As such, penniless relatives who could not afford the expense of transporting the whole family to the gravesite of their departed loved one would pay a smaller charge to a Taoist priest to ferry the dead from one place to another. The priests would lead the Jiangshi to their proper burial ground using magical talismans pinned to the heads of Jiangshi to keep them under control, in a process known as "traveling a corpse over a thousand li." The journey would only be undertaken during the night, and the priest would ring a bell to warn other people of their passing.

Exerting control over larger numbers of Jiangshi would put the strain on magic wielded by the Taoist priests. Consequently, there would be occasions where priests would lose control of the hopping vampires. Driven insane and unable to find their way home, the creature would become wild and unmanageable. In order to regain control, priests would have to use more powerful magical talismans, but getting within close proximity of the vampire was no easy feat. A Jiangshi's strengths lie in its close-range defensive and offensive capabilities, making it impossible for Taoist priests to get close enough to wield their spiritualist magic, leaving the Jiangshi to roam free and cause chaos.

A graveyard in the Shaolin Temple, which serves as a silent testimony to the monk's continuing service to the dead.

The skills afforded by meditation and close-range kung fu techniques made the Shaolin monks the perfect solution to the problem, and so they began to accompany the priests on their journeys. Not only could the monks protect innocent people who were attacked by wayward Jiangshi, they were also able to defend the vampires from bandits and thieves, and ensured they were unharmed before arriving at their final destination.

The Best Offense is a Good Defense

The Shaolin Temple is famous for the profound knowledge and practice of all aspects of martial arts taught therein since the 6th century. Bodhidharma, a Buddhist monk from southern India and the man credited with introducing Chan Buddhism to China, united body and soul in the practices of the Shaolin monks and kick-started their physical training.

According to *The Records of Transmission of the Lamp* (or *Jing de zhuan deng lu*), Bodhidharma arrived in southern China around AD 520 and visited the Shaolin Temple shortly after. He was initially rejected by the monks, and so spent nine years meditating in a cave in the mountains. The monks were so impressed by his devotion that they eventually invited him to enter the temple.

Bodhidharma transformed the monks' lifestyle from one based exclusively on the external arts – rituals and scripture translation – and balanced it with a focus on internal development, deep meditation and natural living.

> A special transmission outside the scriptures.
> No dependence on words and letters.
> Direct pointing to the heart of mankind.
> Seeing into one's nature,
> and attainment of Buddhahood.

This statement, attributed to Bodhidharma, forms the basis of his teachings to the monks at Shaolin. He began educating them about his version of meditation, *dhyana* – the proper concentration of the mind. He found that his students were too weak to sustain their stamina during the intense periods

WEAPON OF CHOICE

While the martial arts have undergone many evolutions over the centuries, the weaponry of the Shaolin vampire hunter has remained largely untouched. Aside from the hunter's command of Shaolin martial arts, he has an arsenal of offensive weaponry at his disposal. Shaolin are famous for their staff-fighting techniques. The staff, or *gun*, is known as the grandfather of weapons in Chinese folklore. Like so many concepts in vampire hunting from Asia, the staff is a multipurpose implement, and can be used in offense, defense, and as a tool for other purposes. As we have come to expect with vampire hunters the world over, each weapon has been carefully considered and only implemented if it had multiple benefits.

A sword carved from the peach tree has long been used by hunters in China to battle Jiangshi because of the powerful properties imbued within the wood, which are believed to drive off evil spirits. Over the years, hunters have added other weapons and accessories to their armories. One popular item among certain hunters is the conical hat. It is unlike other hats of its kind. Carefully crafted to be more aerodynamic, hunters learn how to throw the hats like they would a frisbee. The silver-tipped, sharp edges, coupled with the incredible speed of a spinning blade, are able to deal some degree of damage in battle. Though it will not incapacitate the Jiangshi, hunters will throw the hat as a diversionary tactic. It takes incredible skill to know how to handle the spinning hat, and its lack of dependency in battle is a reason why other hunters may not choose to learn how to master it.

of meditation, and so introduced physical fitness and martial arts into their training in order to strengthen body as well as mind. Bodhidharma stressed the importance of fusing these two practices together to create a whole, perfect warrior. In doing so, the monks were able to harmonize their external body strength with their internal mind strength, thereby invigorating the fundamental life force, *qi*.

Bodhidharma's greatest contribution to what would serve as a Shaolin vampire hunter's most crucial technique almost one thousand years later was *qigong* (chi gung), or "life energy cultivation." The practice comprised three elements: breathing, posture, and the mental focus of guiding *qi* through the body, thereby emphasizing a calm state of mind. Bodhidharma believed that the regulation of one's breath would increase stamina and endurance and allow the monks to become more capable at practicing advanced and difficult martial art techniques.

Taoists held similar beliefs to those of the Buddhist teachings of *qigong*, and the practice adopted by the Shaolin monks became a hybrid of Buddhism and Taoism. As a result, they were able to access higher realms of awareness and push themselves further than they had gone before. The training continued to strengthen the monks, eventually becoming a necessity when bandits came to rob from the temples. During the monks' travels, they would teach, share and develop their skills with those they encountered on the way, disseminating diverse martial arts styles across the country and to the rest of Asia.

Though the Shaolin monks had a history of remaining neutral in politics and times of conflict, when they were called upon by the Taoist priests to help

VUNG FU

The Shaolin vampire hunters settled on moves from three animal styles – snake, monkey and the newly developed praying mantis – to form the vung fu style.

The snake style uses coiling motions in the waist, legs and upper body to create rippling effects, and its yin allows the user to penetrate even the most complicated of defenses with expert precision. It also teaches balance and patience, as the user waits for its prey to come within range, and thus conserves energy.

The flexibility, agility and unpredictable nature of the monkey style allows the user to evade danger by using jumps, flips and rolls. A cheekier style than the others, it is used to taunt an opponent, drawing them closer before attacking quickly with multiple hits.

The praying mantis evolved independently of the original five animal styles. It was created by Wang Lang, one of 18 masters who, sometime in the 13th century, were summoned to the Shaolin Temple to improve the martial arts. The style comprises short-range moves combined with fast and complex footwork to strike at an opponent, with emphasis on the elbows and fingers to attack pressure points. Praying mantis amplifies speed, accentuating fast reflexes, and develops patience. The knowledge of pressure points means that a user can focus their *qi* to heal the body. Praying mantis uses the footwork of the monkey style to form its deadly technique.

All three styles act together to produce quick, sharp moves that can seemingly overcome any defense at close range.

with the transportation of Jiangshi, they had to act, if only to protect those who were at harm. The Taoist *qigong* principles of harmony and balance are essential teachings at Shaolin, and the rise of Jiangshi, with the overabundance of *po*, was in direct opposition to what the monks believed. As such, specialist units of Shaolin monks, created specifically for defending against the Jiangshi, were trained at the temple.

However, the Taoist priests soon learned that the Jiangshi were becoming too unruly, and the task of transporting them (in some cases over hundreds of miles) was not attractive, particularly when they were so at risk. Consequently, control over Jiangshi diminished and the vampire problem began to spread. It was no longer enough for the monks to be defensive fighters. They had to switch to an offensive strategy. They had to become hunters.

The Shaolin breathing techniques taught by Bodhidharma were vital in the fight against the Jiangshi. Not only did they allow the hunters to focus their internal energy and deliver maximum impact against their opponent, but by controlling their breathing, the Shaolin vampire hunters were able to evade detection from the Jiangshi, whose instincts are attuned to the distinct energy left behind by a living person's breath. The breathing technique also rendered the Jiangshi's poisonous breath, one of its greatest weapons, almost useless, as the Shaolin vampire hunters were able to get closer to the vampires than anyone else and remain unaffected by the noxious fumes.

A representation of Bodhidharma, the man credited with introducing Chan Buddhism to China. (SIHASAKPRACHUM / Shutterstock.com)

Bodhidharma's legacy extends beyond the meditative exercises he introduced at the Shaolin Temple in the 6th century. He laid the foundation for what would develop into the five animal styles of kung fu – dragon, tiger, leopard, snake and crane – consisting of roughly 172 moves that, in turn, would give birth to many other styles of fighting. Shaolin martial arts were distributed and shared with other martial art practitioners, becoming an amalgamation of different practices and beliefs.

As the Jiangshi threat rose to prominence in the 16th century, the Shaolin monks decided to combine a number of different animal styles to tackle the unique offensive and defensive abilities of their opponents. Through a combination of observation and consideration, they drew on several elements to create a specialist vampire kung fu style, affectionately named by Westerners as "vung fu."

Though the vung fu was an effective fighting style, it was not enough to execute a Jiangshi. The question remained: how do you kill a seemingly indestructible vampire?

The Power of the Symbol

[Overleaf] For reasons that have never been adequately explained, Hong Kong is a hotbed of Jiangshi activity, receiving nearly ten times the number of reported attacks as would be expected for a city of its size.

The complicated process for disposing of a Jiangshi means that hunters need to acquire an array of skills and teachings to overcome the vampire hordes. In addition to their prowess in martial arts and weaponry, and learning how to focus one's *qi*, it is vital that a Jiangshi hunter is trained to wield Taoist magic. This magic is more about faith than it is waving a wand. "Magic" is an abstract term that has entered popular culture because it is a perplexing art form that the uninitiated are unable to comprehend. Its true name is hidden from us, likely destroyed in the devastation of the Shaolin Temple in the early 20th century.

This magic is represented by *fu*, yellow strips of paper that have ancient symbols written upon them. The use of these talismans dates back to the reign of the Five Emperors of China between circa 2852–2205 BC. Their function is not restricted to handling Jiangshi. They can also be used to repel evil of all kinds and are able to enhance a particular ability or characteristic. It is the spiritual process behind the creation of these talismans that gives them their power.

Fu must be written on yellow paper. The color brings clarity and enlightenment to the spell, allowing it to work to maximum effect. It also helps the creator to focus their *qi*. A series of sacred symbols are written upon each *fu*; the exact use of these symbols depends on the magic one is trying to perform.

Only when the inscriptions are made using the blood of a rooster do they have any effect. The reasons for this comes from a tradition in China to use roosters to drive away evil spirits. As an animal that represents yang, the rooster is also able to counter the abundance of yin that has consumed the Jiangshi host. Blood is a constant factor in life and death, and the red color signifies luck. The blood is also used to represent an oath to both rid the mortal plane of the Jiangshi and to deliver the vampire to its resting place. Modern-day tourists and Jiangshi-hunting enthusiasts must be wary of talismans being sold to the public in the temples around China. These are not effective spells to use on vampires and do not hold the same power of those created by trained Jiangshi hunters or genuine Taoist priests.

The talisman must be pinned to the head of the Jiangshi, freezing the vampire in its tracks and allowing it to be controlled by a bell. Every ring of the bell forces the vampire to hop. Once under the control of the hunter, the Jiangshi must be led to its home village, and magic is used to bind it to its new gravesite.

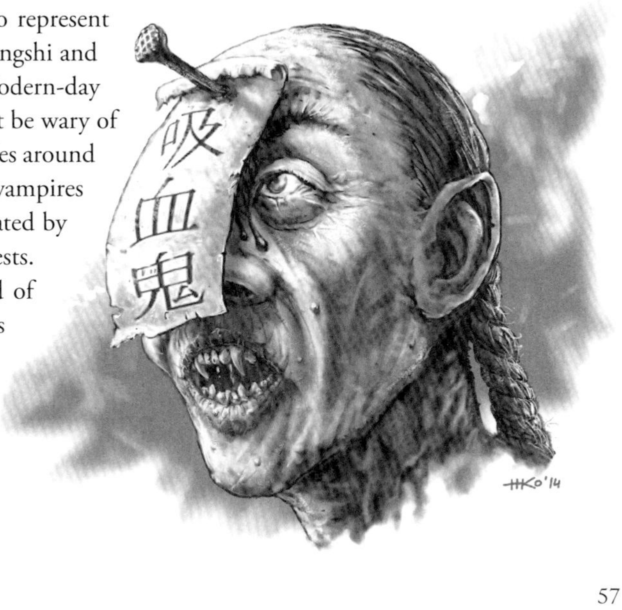

To be fully effective, *fu* must be written on yellow paper. Please note that the symbols reproduced here are representational and should not be used in actual *fu* construction. [Reconstruction by Hauke Kock]

中国料理

The colors on a hunter's costume – white, red, and blue-green – represent concepts that counter a Jiangshi, acting as a defensive layer and helping the hunter to focus their *qi*. White signifies purity and mourning, red is happiness and joy, and blue-green represents spring and vitality. These concepts oppose those represented by the Jiangshi: fear, death, and suffering.

There are a number of other defenses that can be used against a Jiangshi that will pacify the creature for a short period of time. Throwing rice, seeds or dried peas onto the ground will slow the vampire's approach as it stops to count the grains. If backed into a corner, a useful delaying tactic is to create a circle of rice around yourself or the Jiangshi, which will hold the creature at bay. While the rice has no actual physical or mystical power, the creature is hardwired to stop and count the grains of rice.

A hen's egg can slow a Jiangshi (the egg represents new life and we have already noted what effect the chicken family has on the vampire) and loud noises can scare away the vampire. Using a straw broom to literally sweep away a Jiangshi is a common piece of advice that, strange as it may seem, does work. The broom has no real significance; however, it has been given symbolic value as a result of its appearance in folklore tales, which are hundreds of years old. The beliefs in these superstitions have given the broom the power to ward off vampires. It is not the most effective of defenses, but it has some intrinsic value to the masses of Chinese citizens who possess one of these objects, offering assurance that they hold some sort of protection against the invasion of Jiangshi.

Monks practice *kung fu* in this ancient mural from the Shaolin Temple. Eventually the monks repurposed many of the elements from different *kung fu* forms to aid in the fight against vampires. (Alamy)

The Jiangshi is a nocturnal being, and a "fresh" creature, recently risen from its grave, can be killed by the sunlight, having yet to become strong enough to withstand the rays. However, as the vampire becomes more powerful, the sun's effect lessens, and it will become an inanimate, statue-like corpse in the sunlight, reverting back to its vampire state when night returns. This is a useful method for holding a fully-developed Jiangshi in place during the day, though it will not kill it.

As a Jiangshi spends more time outside of the grave, it grows more intelligent and evil. At the peak of its evolution, a Jiangshi can be identified by its long, white hair and eyebrows, increased speed, greater ease of movement, and ability to jump higher and longer distances. Eyewitnesses claim to have seen Jiangshi levitate and even fly, but it is merely their skill in jumping that creates this illusion of flight.

Decapitation, cremation and lightning are the only ways to completely destroy a Jiangshi. The former is the preferred method among vampire hunters, as it is also the simplest. It is difficult to predict when and where lightning will occur, and it is the reason why Jiangshi are so afraid of loud noises, as thunder often indicates lightning. A drum is the most effective tool for generating this noise, and so many hunters choose to carry a small *ganngu* drum. Although vampire hunters are able to choose a less violent path to lay a Jiangshi to rest – using Taoist magic, a hunter could lead a Jiangshi to its familial home and inter the vampire using the proper burial rites – due to the effort and time it would take to perform this method, it was and still is very rarely undertaken.

Weaponizing Emotions

As the Shaolin vampire hunters became more skilled and experienced in dealing with vampires, they would pass on their learnings to other parts of the East, just as their predecessors did. Lines of communication became more established and hunters from Japan and India told tales of vampires from their native countries.

A talent that is often associated with the vampire is a mystical allure that it uses to ensnare its victims. Popular vampiric fiction relates fantasies of suave, sophisticated and desirable vampires that seductively swoop in to hypnotise young victims. In reality, this technique – known as glamoring – is less amplified, but compelling nonetheless. The powerful persuasive technique allows vampires to delve deep into the human psyche and prey on victims' emotions. In actuality, vampires are using a type of low-level psychic control, or extrasensory perception, to project an illusion into the minds of victims.

The ability to shapeshift is common among descriptions of vampire encounters in Asia. Popularly, Jiangshi choose to present themselves as wolves when projecting shapeshifting images of themselves. Although vampires are traditionally linked to bats, the flying mammal is revered in China, and its Chinese translation – *fu* – is a homophone for the word for good fortune. The bat has represented luck and good fortune for centuries, and so it does not carry the same negative connotations as it does elsewhere. Psychic vampires such as these want to feed off extreme and raw human emotion.

Where Jiangshi attacks are concerned, women are more at risk than men. Driven by their strong desire, Jiangshi will gravitate towards female victims for before attempting to ingest their *qi*. This is a result of the po's effect on the Jiangshi. The desire is extended to other vampire types in the East, such as the Indian Rakshasa and the Filipino Aswang, who present themselves as beautiful women to attract unsuspecting men.

The Aswang is a particularly ferocious creature, and is able to roam day and night to find prey. It favors the blood of children and seems to transform itself into an animal, such as a dog, cat or bird, to entice young victims. When it has taken its prey, it might replace the body with a corpse or a doppelganger that it has crafted.

Humans in Japan must be especially careful, as the native Gaki vampire chooses to impersonate living people, appearing as a loved one to evoke powerful feelings. These vampires are perhaps even more deadly, preying not on fear, but the love – and, in some cases, desire – of their prey to trap their victim.

Vampire hunters in Asian countries are specially trained to deal with this psychic interference by focusing their *qi* and clearing their minds of emotion. They must be unwavering in their determination and aims, and they cannot let the allure of the vampire's illusion and attempted penetration of their psyche distract them from the task at hand.

To this day, the Shaolin vampire hunters remain a highly specialist unit of vampire killer. No other hunting group in the world can match their skill, focus and discipline. While they have tried to disseminate their teachings across the continent of Asia, too few people are able successfully to commit to the training and achieve the level of proficiency that is required, and this breed of vampire hunter is still too scarce.

A statue of an Indian Rakshasa. Experts are still arguing whether this creature should be classified as a vampire or a demon. (J Marshall - Tribaleye Images / Alamy)

Though the hunters in China are managing to curb the spread of Qing-Dynasty Jiangshi across the country, no amount of Shaolin skill or Taoist magic is able to stem the spiritual transformation process, and Jiangshi continue to rise.

As transportation has developed, particularly during the 1900s, more and more Chinese citizens have moved out of the country and spread out across the globe. If these people are not properly honored in death, we may bear witness to the rise of a new wave of 20th-century-style Jiangshi in communities that are completely unqualified to deal with the threat. It is imperative that the Shaolin vampire hunters act now to impart their expertise on an international level to prepare us for the future. Time is against us, and the survival of the deadly Jiangshi seems inevitable.

Who's laughing now?

[1] Other accepted variations of Jiangshi include *kyong-shi* (Japanese), *geungshi* (Cantonese) and *gangshi* (Korean).

Chapter 5 - South American Vampires

A Brief History

The evolution of vampirism in South America stems back to the Ice Age and, unlike most other continents, has little that relates to the preternatural or paranormal. It is, in fact, tied closely to vampire bats and the migration of megafauna.

Vampire bats have been closely associated with their vampire namesakes for centuries and have become increasingly common as a result of the vast herds of livestock they feed on in North and South America. The oldest fossil vampire bat dates back around three million years, to the Upper Pliocene Period of Florida, and many fossil species are much larger than their modern relatives. *Desmodus draculae* is a quarter larger than the extant common vampire bat, *Desmodus rotundus*, and some fossils are associated with the animals they were presumably feeding on, such as rhino-sized ground sloths found in Brazil complete with bat remains.

During the last Ice Age, which ended some 12,000 years ago, the formation of massive polar ice caps resulted in a drop in sea levels that led to the formation of numerous land bridges, including the Isthmus of Panama. This allowed animal populations to migrate between the continents; in the case of South America, a number of mammal groups arrived, including elephants, camels, horses and big cats, known collectively as megafauna. Naturally, they brought their parasites with them, including vampire bats.

There were a number of physically large animal groups already in South America, so the bats soon made themselves at home. At this point in their evolution, one lineage of vampire bats chose a different path to their contemporaries that would lead to their ultimate expression in what is known to vampire hunters and cryptozoologists around the world as the Chupacabra.

This ancient statue of a bat-god hints at the long relationship between the Chupacabra and the early Mesoamericans. (age fotostock / Alamy)

The Yucatan Peninsula of Mexico is riddled with a system of around 6,000 caves and sinkholes known as cenotes, the largest of which is 200ft (60 meters) across and 100ft (30 meters) deep. These are the result of millions of years of dissolution of the limestone bedrock that makes up the Yucatán, leading to the formation of vast underground aquifers. The water in these cenotes has allowed rich, fertile jungles to grow and provided a home for the invading megafauna. The vampire bats took up residence in the many sinkholes and caves permeating the region, and it was here that they began to adapt to their new environment.

Already larger than contemporary vampire bats, the Chupacabra lineage also changed its hunting style. Many animals would come to the cenotes to drink at night, so the vampires found they no longer needed to fly the distances required of their relatives. Not surprisingly, they also undertook a rather radical behavioral change, becoming swimmers (probably by accident). Considering the prevalence of water in their chosen environment, this was a logical step, as was the development of their climbing abilities. Bats have always been good climbers, scrabbling around on rock faces, but the Chupacabra took it a stage further. Muscle groups designed for flying and climbing grew in strength, and wings designed for flying adapted to swimming. They could still fly, but it became less important – usually just a method of migrating from one cenote to another.

Spending so much time in the water and living in a generally benign climate resulted in the Chupacabra swapping fur for a fine layer of down, giving them an almost albino-like appearance.

Another, rather unpleasant, adaptation was using ammonia as a largely defensive weapon. Ammonia is a waste by-product of digesting blood; when attacked, the Chupacabra has been known to spray foul-smelling faecal ammonia, which is similar to being violently dosed with smelling salts.

Desmodus rotundus, more commonly known as the vampire bat, is the ancient ancestor of the Chupacabra. (Alessandro Catenazz)

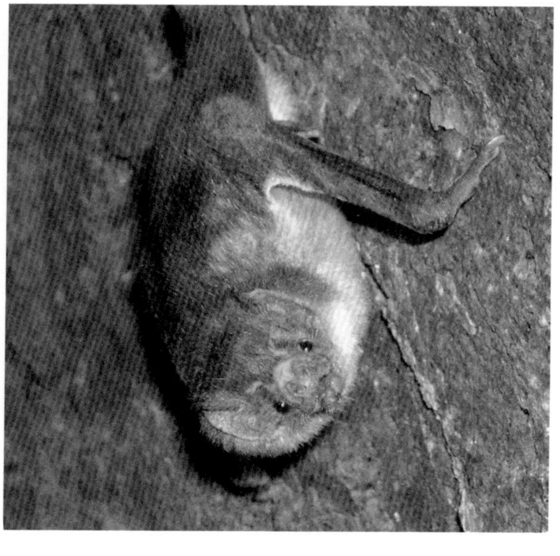

As such, by the end of the last Ice Age, they were radically different from their small, flittering ancestral forms, and were given the scientific name *Megalodesmodus cenotesensis* – the "giant vampire bat of the cenotes."

However, the end of the Ice Age heralded the catastrophic mass extinction of the American megafauna, depriving the Chupacabra of its principal prey. Massive environmental change was no doubt instrumental in the destruction of the megafauna, but there is a great deal of suspicion levelled at *Homo sapiens*, who had first arrived in the Americas about 21,000 years ago. Hunting cultures, using advanced flint spearheads, were hunting even the largest mammoths at this time, and may have contributed to their downfall.

Mesoamerican Religion

Nothing remains historically (or prehistorically) of the first interactions between early Americans and the Chupacabra, but around 7,000 years ago humans began to settle in Central America as farmers. We can only surmise on the impact the Chupacabra had on the belief systems of the earliest known Mesoamericans, such as the Olmecs, going back to around 1200 BC. All their religions are based on blood and water, often one symbolically representing the other.

For the Mayans, the northernmost part of their empire was the Yucatán Peninsula. It was they who probably first encountered the Chupacabra, using as they did the cenotes to water their crops. This required farmers and workers to go into the caves, where they almost certainly fell victim to the vampires. The cenotes were additionally seen as entrances to the Mayan underworld of the dead, a place also associated with bats. According to Mayan religion, the bats gave off terrible shrieks – possibly an interpretation of the Chupacabra's high-pitched sonar it uses to navigate in the enclosed caves and also under water. Similarly, two lords of the Mayan Underworld, House Corner and Blood Gatherer, were blood drinkers, attacking the neck and other vulnerable areas of the poor souls traveling through this Mesoamerican hell.

At some point in their history, Mayans began making blood sacrifices in the cenotes, as well as gathering water from them. These offerings may have started as a way of distracting or placating the Chupacabras, but soon the vampires became deified and the offering ritualized, the Mayans decapitating their victims. Chupacabra attacks rarely managed this, but their attacks were focused around the face and neck, so it is not too surprising that the Mayans would focus on the same areas.

An adult male Chupacabra, drawn from the only specimen known to have been captured alive, currently believed to be housed somewhere in New Mexico. (Reconstruction by Hauke Kock)

(Opposite) Many South American hunters who specialize in fighting Chupacabras still employ traditional methods and modes of dress on their hunts.

Much of surviving Mayan writing interweaves history and mythology, making it difficult for vampire scholars to determine the facts, but there is clearly a link between blood and water. The Mesoamericans even used fish bones to let blood in as a form of autosacrifice. The moment of death was compared to the sensation of sinking into water; for those sacrificed to the cenotes, this would have been a very literal interpretation. Seashells, fish and water lilies often adorn representations of the Mayan underworld, Xibalba.

The Chupacabras themselves seem to have been mainly located in the northwest of the Yucatán Peninsula, in what the Mayans called The Land of Deer and Turkey, a region thick with swamps and marshes, where the locals grew cacao and where, no doubt, many of the farmers fell victim to vampire attacks.

The Aztecs, whose empire was even more powerful but further north, took the symbolism of blood and water even further. The rain gods were fed blood by the shooting of arrows into human sacrifices, the blood then drizzled onto the ground to encourage fertility and plentiful rain. One of their principal gods, Quetzalcoatl, was revered as a dragon-like feathered serpent and was associated with storms, wind, and blood sacrifice. Vampire scholars have speculated (and again, there is no evidence one way or the other) that Chupacabras are not unlike small dragons; it also may be no coincidence that they often use storms to cover their attacks, their senses unimpeded by rain and thunder.

An Aztec blood-sacrifice. The connection between ancient Mesoamerican religion, blood-sacrifice, and the Chupacabra is a slowly expanding field of research. (North Wind Picture Archives / Alamy)

Another Aztec deity was Mictlantecuhtli, the ruler of the Atzec underworld, Mictlan. He was believed to have huge, dead eyes and a horrible grin, large clawed hands, was desperately skinny and had lost half of his flesh. Worship of Mictlantecuhtli was more usually associated with cannibalism and the Aztec underworld more closely related to dogs, but the description and images of the underworld ruler could quite easily have been modeled on a Chupacabra. The wonderfully bizarre headdresses of Aztec royalty and officials also seem to mimic in some ways the strange nasal folds and ears of the vampires.

Whether the Aztecs had direct contact with the Chupacabras is unknown; much of their religion was derived from that of earlier Mesoamericans, including the Mayans, so the links to bloodletting may be entirely

coincidental. However, there is evidence that the Chupacabra population was already spreading north up into what is now Mexico during the "classic" period of Mesoamerican history. This was no doubt the result of increased food availability, either as a result of blood sacrifices being made directly to them or by increased amounts of prey, in the form of humans. Inferred evidence also indicates they spread south out of the Yucatán in the 9th century, descending into the lowlands at a time when many Mayan city states there were collapsing. The human population is reckoned to have dropped a third during the course of that century, possibly as a result of intense farming and overpopulation, triggering an environmental disaster. This instigated a period of open war between the cities as they struggled to survive, battling for land and for prisoners to be offered as blood sacrifices to gods the Mayans believed were now displeased.

The impact on Chupacabra numbers can only be guessed. Never particularly numerous and built for stealth, they also moved solely at night, while many of their attacks may have been mistaken for the work of jaguars or pumas, or even the much smaller vampire bats. As such, a census of numbers and distribution is impossible to create. What is left is guesswork, mostly garnered from reports drafted by the Spanish Conquistadors, who arrived in Central America in 1519, shattering the world of the Mesoamericans forever.

Blood and Steel

To many Aztecs, Hernán Cortés seemed like Quetzalcoatl himself, whose return had been foretold in Aztec legend. Wearing metal armor and astride the first horses to enter South America since the end of the Ice Age, he and his companions must have seemed godlike, but the Spaniards (actually Castilians) were after gold and slaves while spreading Catholicism, the two often going hand in hand. After attempts at diplomacy, appeasement and witchcraft failed to placate the erstwhile invaders, Aztec emperor, Montezuma, decided they had to be stopped by force.

The Aztec elite fighters were the Eagle and Jaguar warriors, who could only adorn themselves as their namesakes after proving their fearlessness in battle. However, Mesoamerican warfare was usually less about killing and more about the taking of prisoners to feed the voracious appetites of the human-sacrificing priests. As such, when they first came up against the cannons and small arms, swords and armor of the Conquistadors, they stood very little chance. The Castilians were further aided by treachery and smallpox, and soon the Aztec empire had been brought to its knees.

The end of the Mayans was not so easy. Politically and socially, they were more diverse, with no godhead such as Montezuma to be removed, thereby undermining the nation. The Mayans fought a guerrilla war in thick jungle from 1518 until the last pocket of resistance was crushed in 1697, while across Central America a terrifying combination of drought and outbreaks of

European diseases such as typhus, influenza and most infamously, smallpox, wiped out almost 80 percent of the region's population.

This was equally disastrous for the Chupacabras, whose reliance on blood sacrifice meant their primary food source was gone, while the drought drove them deep underground.

Then, around 1523, the Conquistadors arrived on the Yucatán, and with them the Catholic clergy who saw to their administrative as well as spiritual needs, and Hispanicized Europeans. The latter were from areas familiar with vampirism in its truer forms and what many of the Conquistadors saw as blood-soaked idolatry these Europeans saw as vampire attack. The decision was taken to clean out the threat.

Wily and pragmatic, the invaders were never averse to the hiring of defeated locals to join their army as auxiliaries, and a number of the surviving Aztec elite, perhaps equally pragmatic and realistic, were formed up into units that were sent into the cenotes, nicknamed Mictlans after the Aztec underworld.

Records are spotty about what happened next. Much information was lost due to deliberate misinformation by the Conquistadors in documents being sent back to the royal courts as part of an ongoing campaign to fox Spain's colonial competitor, Portugal. Moreover, what information did make it back to the Inquisition was often disregarded as the work of perfectly natural predators such as jaguars and, as mentioned previously, vampire bats.

However, there were certain documents that made their way to the Vatican via spies and informants, some of which caused concern and led to the clergy operating alongside the Conquistadors to take on the role of the Inquisition and hunt down this new vampire menace.

Female Chupacabras are smaller and have slightly larger ears but are just as vicious. (Reconstruction by Hauke Kock)

Expeditions utilizing auxiliary warriors, especially Aztec and Mayan forces, and led by the Hispanicized Europeans, both soldiers and priests, descended into the cenotes. These first missions were disasters. Religious icons and symbols were a matter of supreme indifference to the Chupacabras and when the Conquistadors tried burning out the vampires they simply fled into the water. Some of the expeditions became lost or disorientated and ended up finding themselves prey to the hungry Chupacabras, already culturally adapted to the hunting of humans.

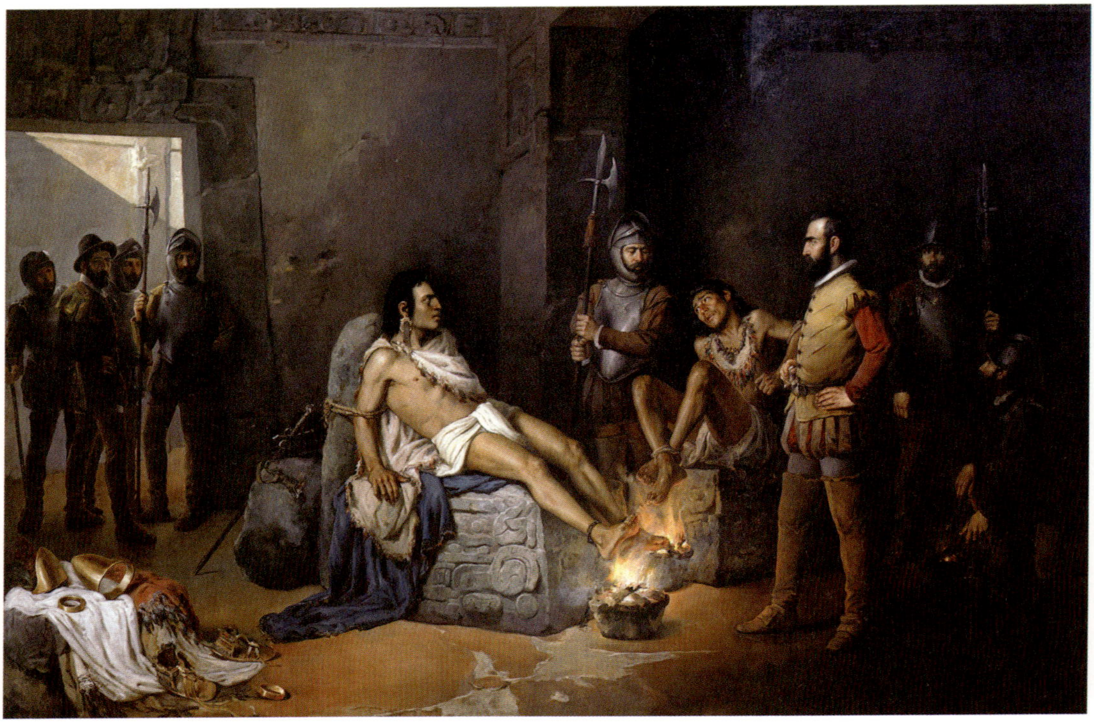

Conquistadors torture an Aztec. Such torture was used to reveal the location of many Chupacabra groups. (The Art Archive / Alamy)

However, a few of the vampires were killed and the academics amongst the clergy had a chance to take a look at the perceived threat. It became clear that these were nothing like the vampires encountered by some of the expedition members in Europe. While adapting to a life underground had given them a certain photosensitivity, the Chupacabras were not in any way vulnerable to sunlight like European vampires. This, and the failure of Christian weapons, led the expedition leaders to conclude that these were just highly evolved vermin, more harmful than a man-eating jaguar, but clearly no longer requiring the resources of the Inquisition and clergy. As such, the destruction of the Chupacabra lairs was made a military matter.

The first thing the Conquistadors did was bring in Molossers, tough war dogs that had terrified the Mesoamericans in battle. The ammonia stench of the vampires was easy enough for humans to follow, but the dogs could smell the lairs even amidst the mélange of smells generated by the sweltering rainforest.

They also brought boats into the cenotes. Using fire to drive the Chupacabras into the water, they would then be lanced by native warriors, proficient with atlatls, spear-throwers that could accurately cast javelins a great distance.

Sometimes, the Chupacabras could be coaxed above ground with staked-out bait, such as a goat, donkey, or occasionally, harking back to the religious belief of the Mesoamericans, a child. The hungry vampires would risk exposure above ground at the possibility of an easy meal, and paid for it with their lives.

Gone North

The Conquistador extermination program lasted barely a year, but was effective enough to wipe out the Chupacabras of the Yucatán. By 1524, the Spaniards were establishing themselves across the peninsula and the few remaining Chupacabras seemed to have scattered into the southern lowlands before turning northwest and migrating slowly up the Isthmus of Panama.

Studies by UNESCO indicate they were surprisingly adaptable and resilient. There were plenty of jungles and waterways for them to disappear into, but there was a lack of large prey. As such, they were drawn to human settlements, feeding on livestock and the occasional unlucky human; it also seems they became scavengers, an easy way to find food at a time when disease was devastating the indigenous populations of the region. Few in number, and with few humans to notice, the Chupacabras' passage north went largely unobserved.

Their fortunes changed when Francisco Vásquez de Coronado set out in search of gold in southern North America, bringing with him herds of cattle. Some of the vampires shadowed the expedition through the deserts of the region, living off the blood of the occasional stray, eating the dead and taking the occasional live human victim.

The sparsely populated regions of Central and southern North America allowed the Chupacabra populations to establish new bridgeheads. The rugged, mountainous terrain, limestone cave systems, empty deserts, and thick forest all provided havens, and as cattle farming took a hold in the region, the vampires found new prey. Even so, these were tough environments and their numbers were never able to swell to anything like those of the Yucatán. They disappeared from sight and, as such, the Yucatán vampires more or less vanished into myth and legend.

How far north they traveled has become a matter of debate. UNESCO vampire units were on hand during the cattle mutilation scares of the 1970s. Some of these took place as far north as South Dakota. Evidence of Chupacabra involvement is circumstantial, but the report of strange medicinal smells around the carcasses of the victims could indicate the presence of ammonia. There were also reports of unusual footprints around the bodies, not unlike suction cups. Chupacabra are "knuckle walkers" and could quite easily account for these unusual punch holes in the ground. Perhaps most significant was the complete exsanguination of many of the animals involved, and the apparent application of an anticoagulant to expedite this. Like their ancestral bat forms, Chupacabras possess a natural anticoagulant in their saliva.

The causes of many of these cattle mutilations (which also involve horses and other livestock) remain the source of much conjecture and conspiracy theories, but UNESCO, in a report in 1985, did conclude that there was strong evidence in some cases of vampirism by *Megalodesmodus*.

Much stronger evidence of Chupacabra attacks came from their old hunting ground in Central America and led ultimately to the informal term for the species. In 1995, a number of sheep were killed, and exsanguinated, in Puerto Rico. Soon after came reports of the cryptid that became known as the Chupacabra, the "goat sucker." The early descriptions immediately drew the interest of UNESCO's vampire unit. While there was no doubt some hysteria and sensationalism was involved in many of the sightings, there was enough solid evidence to support a sudden rise in the threat level posed by the vampire. Many of the reports of strange, naked-skinned animals with bizarre limb proportions were attributed to dogs or coyotes with *Sarcoptes scabiei*, better known as itch mites, which cause fur loss and unpleasant and unsightly rashes. In serious cases, the infected animal can look almost naked.

A number of reported Chupacabra specimens happened to have been eaten by vultures or such, or have turned out to indeed be coyotes. Two were allegedly shot by animal control officers in Hood County in 2010, but nothing further was heard about these and they have been secured by UNESCO.

Sightings of the vampire have occurred as far north as Maine, but are centered mainly in the southern US and northern Mexico. However, there is now increasing evidence of a Chupacabra presence in major cities, using the new underground network generated by sewers and storm drains. How long they have been there is unknown, but they so far do not constitute an infestation. UNESCO vampirism officials have been conducting investigations (often posing as sewer workers or even vagrants) to assess the extent of the problem, but many of the cities suspected of harboring Chupacabras have hundreds of miles of tunnels that are many centuries old, and the cities are teeming with plentiful food supplies. Cities where a presence has been positively identified include Los Angeles, New York (specifically Manhattan), Chicago, Dallas, Denver, Mexico City and Tijuana.

However, the presence of Chupacabras remains a low priority for UNESCO and the SAU units. As the vampires do not pass on the condition as Strigoi do, they are considered a minor threat, at least for now. But the true size of the problem remains to be seen and will only become clear on completion of the UNESCO survey. In the meantime, there are many in SAU who feel prevention is better than cure, and already expeditions have been mounted into the sewers of New York, Chicago and Mexico City to develop tactics in eliminating any possible future threat. Many of these are modeled on the Conquistadors and their Mesoamerican vassals.

CONCLUSION

THE VAMPIRE WARS

Thanks in part to the activities of the North American vampire, species of vampire are no longer confined to the areas they had inhabited for millennia. With Europe traditionally considered the epicenter of vampire activity, who would suspect the central power base to be relocated to a region with so little vampire history?

The enormous fortunes that the Old World vampires of Europe brought with them when they immigrated to North America were invested in steel, the railway and communications. With a powerful hold on these commercial areas, the North American vampires have not only become wealthy, they have also been able to open the lines of communication and transportation, leading to a prolific dissemination and networking of the vampire species.

This gruesome sketch serves as a reminder that, at their most basic, vampires are animalistic predators who view the mass of humanity as little more than cattle. (Bridgeman Art Library)

With clear and established lines of communication and leadership – and with very little opposition – the immigrant North American vampires are leading the offensive against humanity. Vampires have been spreading across the globe for decades, particularly to North America where a lack of true vampire history has resulted in little skill and demand for hunting. Consequently, the congregations of species that have gathered there have been allowed to breed unheeded and in relative peace.

But these New World vampires are not relying solely on their wealth and power to attract other vampire covens to build up their empire. There are those species that possess a limited and primal intelligence, who do not have the mental capacity to be driven by such materialistic reward. As such, it is

(Previous) There is no doubt that vampires are now more organized than ever before. There will likely come a day when all vampire hunters around the world will be called together to fight in defense of humanity.

believed that the North American vampire leaders are exploiting the psychic and empathic abilities showcased by the Chinese Jiangshi and the African Obayifo to influence other, more susceptible vampires into joining their ranks.

There is evidence, for example, that the South American Chupacabra is penetrating the major cities across the North American continent. This behavior is not consistent with historical records of the Chupacabra – they have never been known to approach such densely populated and modern areas, and yet the evidence that more and more of their number are driving further north is increasing month on month. Inhabiting the maze of sewers beneath these metropolises, it is suspected that the Chupacabras are answering the call of their "masters," vampires who are thought to be using a combination of low-level psychic resonance and echolocation to summon their brethren. Moreover, with numbers of Chupacabra having plummeted in recent years, could the North American vampire be trying to propagate the species? It seems the vampires are using whatever they have at their disposal in order to build their forces.

From the Vatican to UNESCO

For more than 500 years, the Vatican led the fight against vampires in Europe. It was they who took on the formalized and organized hunting of vampires, with their first officially sanctioned engagement with the Strigoi taking place in 1520, though the task forces to counter the threat had been in the works long before that. In the early centuries AD, warrior priests had trained in the local monasteries. But over time, as the threats worsened, these young hunters

The Vatican library, home of the famous "Z Collection," one of the world's largest repositories for knowledge about the undead, including vampires. (Francesco Dazzi / Shutterstock.com)

that were working alone to destroy the enemy in their respective European communities became less effective.

Consequently, the Vatican acted to bring together resources from across the continent to better organize the attacks on the vampires, a move that would be mirrored some 500 years later.

Due to the proliferation of new, previously unknown species of vampires appearing in different countries and continents, the Vatican-sanctioned teams were unable to keep up with their offensive. They recognized that the traditional weapons and tactics used by the European hunters were not enough to tackle the various threats. Subsequently, UNESCO assumed responsibility for dealing with the vampire menace on a global scale. Just as the Vatican brought together the hunters from across Europe, UNESCO has been able to do the same on an international level.

UNESCO was founded shortly after the end of World War II, on November 16, 1945. It aims to encourage collaboration between nations through education, science and culture, in order to establish a peaceful world order. As part of the United Nations, the organization is able to bring all the relevant national parties together in relative privacy, averting the gaze from those prying eyes that would incite mass panic.

As UNESCO aimed to amass the specialist knowledge and skills from each area of the globe in order to inform and educate other hunters, they employed new teams, dubbed Special Action Units (SAU). The SAUs sought to understand everything possible about the vampires in order to counter any possible threat.

The UNESCO world headquarters in Paris, the center for antivampire activities in the modern world. (Simon Tranter Photography / Alamy)

For example, vampires like the Jiangshi have the potential to emerge almost anywhere on Earth. Therefore, it is vital for the Shaolin vampire hunters to share their knowledge of the spiritualist side of hunting, which far exceeds that of any other hunter in the world.

Furthermore, the skills of the Ghanaian hunter and his African brothers are crucial learnings in the North American urban jungles that are currently witnessing vampire uprisings. These new North American opponents may differ from the forest-based threats, such as the Asanbosam, but the African hunters are able to use their abilities to reach places other hunters cannot. They can exercise these talents, which resemble the art of *parkour* (a modern-day version of the skills developed by the hunters hundreds of years ago in the African forests), itself developed from military obstacle course training.

A rare photograph of Telsa Dane, "The Louisiana Vampire." Telsa disappeared from her Baton Rouge mental hospital in 2008 before experts could determine the true nature of her apparent vampirism.

As such, training camps are currently being established at key locations across the world, where vital individuals from all continents are pulling together to impart their skills and knowledge and plan their assault. In addition, the work between these new inquisitors and several highly classified US military units in the late 1990s and early 2000s has helped to prepare them for combat in the field. Those relationships between UNESCO and North America are proving vital as we move closer to all-out war with the vampires.

Faith is the connecting thread throughout this guide. The religious traditions have always been a part of the counter-vampire culture, no matter the country of origin. Every task force is laced with religious iconography and a symbolic belief that has helped them to overcome their opponents. It seems that even before UNESCO stepped in, the hunters were writing chapters from the same book. Now it is up to UNESCO to ensure that they complete the story – to create the most successful and efficient antivampire units the world has ever seen.

A New Age Dawns

The translation of traditional hunting tactics and vampire knowledge from the Old World sites in Europe, Asia and Africa to those hunters stationed in the New World areas would be an impossible task without the latest advancements in communication. Now, the few vampire hunters that exist in North America are looking to assimilate knowledge and skills from their transatlantic kin.

In the 1970s and 1980s, UNESCO embarked on a plan to address the imbalance in global communication. Establishing a set of communication channels where media would flow freely, UNESCO is in a better position to identify vampire communications. In addition, with new recommendations in place, UNESCO is able to encourage and nurture cross-communication of the vampire hunting techniques, allowing the knowledge to cross-pollinate around the globe.

Like the vampires, hunters have worked independently of each other for centuries, in most cases taking a reactive approach to hunting by simply repelling more immediate and localized threats. Now that the vampires' power base has shifted from Europe to North America, and as the vampire groups evolve from unruly sects to organized armies, so must the hunters move to the source of the upcoming conflicts and become more proactive in their attacks.

As we continue into the 21st century, the art of war is changing. Technology is affecting the global landscape, and so the hunters must learn to adapt and develop their skills to meet the new demands. Medieval techniques need to be communicated, embraced and brought up to date so that today's hunters have the potential to overpower the resilient vampires of the Old World.

Vampires have carried out a number of criminal activities to fund their ever-expanding empire and secure their grip on North America. Human trafficking, prostitution, drugs – these activities were conveniently overlooked by law

Modern hunters must be ready to combat any variety of vampire. This is most true for hunters in Asia, who have lately seen a large influx of European or American Strigoi.

enforcement, with any investigation immediately stalled as a result of random killings or the timely intervention of corrupt cops. But now these movements are being caught on camera.

Technological improvements in communication are not only helping both vampire and hunter factions to amass, they are transforming the once-secret war into a public broadcast. With the explosion of camera phones and social media (not to mention the ever-growing presence of mass media) the vampires' clandestine operations are now being uncovered for the world to see.

Spurred on by the suggestion that vampires do indeed exist, thrill-seeking, naïve youngsters are taking it upon themselves to hunt down and document vampire activity, and various social media channels and blogs are dedicated to the pursuit of evidence. Despite the number of fatal injuries and killings resulting from these intrusions, delusional youths and documentary filmmakers continue to take to the streets in order to penetrate the underbelly of the vampire underworld and capture the next great vampire selfie.

Authorities in those countries where this documentation is being published are forced by wealthy and powerful pro-vampire supporters to conceal any vampire activity that appears online in an effort to shield their movements. Vampires have surveillance all over the global communications network, pulling down information from the Internet as soon as it goes up. Though they act as quickly as possible, will they be able to keep up with the pace of this fast-moving technological world before the secret is well and truly out? And will the transmission of all this easily accessible information help or hinder the vampire hunting community? It is too soon to tell.

The changing face of the human-vampire war does not simply represent a shift to the technological: as the vampires and the hunters come together in their respective groups to build and train their forces, the hunters are blending the spiritual, psychological and intellectual elements together. Confronted with this ever-changing landscape, the importance of the guide you hold in your hands has never been greater.

We are entering a new age of vampire hunting. As the Old World and the New World unite, the spiritual experience of being a hunter is aligning with the approaches of the modern world. It is imperative that we act now and prepare ourselves for what is to come, for the sake of the human race.

Have you got what it takes?

Glossary

COINCIDENCE A concurrence of events without apparent causal connection.

COMMITTED To send someone to be confined in a psychiatric hospital.

CONSECRATE To make something sacred.

CORROBORATE To confirm or give support to.

MASSACRE Intentionally killing a large number of people.

DELUSION An impression that is believed despite being contradicted by what is generally accepted as reality.

DEMONIC Characteristic of demons or evil spirits.

FORMIDABLE Inspiring fear or respect through being powerful.

INFESTATION Invaded or overrun by organisms or beings.

LUMINESCENCE The emission of light by a substance.

MANIFESTATION A display or demonstration by an act or appearance.

MELANCHOLY A feeling of sadness, usually with no obvious cause.

METAMORPHOSIS A smooth change from one form to another.

NOTORIOUS Famous for some bad quality.

PARANORMAL Beyond the scope of normal scientific understanding.

POSSESSED Controlled by an evil spirit.

PRETERNATURAL Beyond what is normal or natural.

TELEPATHY Communication of thoughts or ideas by means other than the known senses.

THEORIZE To create a theoretical premise or framework for something.

For More Information

American Society for Psychical Research, Inc. (ASPR)
5 West 73rd Street
New York, NY 10023
(212) 799-5050
Website: http://www.aspr.com

This organization's mission is to explore extraordinary or unexplained phenomena that have been called psychic or paranormal and their implications for our understanding of consciousness, the universe, and the nature of existence. It addresses questions with scientific research and offers educational activities, including lectures and conferences.

Ghost Hunters
Syfy Channel
NBCUniversal Cable Entertainment Group
30 Rockefeller Plaza
New York, NY 10112
(212) 664-4444
Website: http://www.syfy.com/ghosthunters

In each episode of the *Ghost Hunters* television program, Jason Hawes and his team of paranormal investigators, TAPS (The Atlantic Paranormal Society) investigate paranormal activity across the country.

Rhine Research Center
2741 Campus Walk Avenue
Building 500
Durham, NC 27705
(919) 309-4600
Website: http://rhinecenter.org

The Rhine Research Center's mission is to advance the science of parapsychology, to provide education and resources for the public, and to foster a community for individuals with personal and professional interest in paranormal phenomena and the nature of human consciousness.

TAPS *ParaMagazine*
PO Box 233
Fly Creek, NY 13337
jvj@tapsparamag.com
Website: www.tapsparamag.com
Founded by The Atlantic Paranormal Society (TAPS) in 2008, *ParaMagazine* is America's premiere paranormal print and digital publication featuring the top minds on the topics of paranormal investigations, cryptozoology, ufology, and spiritual beliefs.

Websites

Because of the changing nature of internet links, Rosen Publishing has developed an online list of websites related to the subject of this book. This site is updated regularly. Please use this link to access the list:

http://www.rosenlinks.com/MH/vampires

For Further Reading

Buckland, Raymond. *The Weiser Field Guide to Ghosts: Apparitions, Spirits, Spectral Lights, and Other Hauntings of History and Legend.* San Francisco, CA: Weiser Books, 2009.

Garden, Joe, and Miles Proctor. *The New Vampire's Handbook: A Guide For The Recently Turned Creature of the Night.* New York, NY: Villard Books, 2009.

Gibson, Marley, Patrick Burns, and Dave Schrader. *The Other Side: A Teen's Guide to Ghost Hunting and the Paranormal.* Boston, MA: Houghton Mifflin Harcourt, 2009.

Guiley, Rosemary. *The Encyclopedia of Vampires & Werewolves.* New York, NY: Facts On File, 2011.

Horn, Stacy. *Unbelievable: Investigations into Ghosts, Poltergeists, Telepathy, and Other Unseen Phenomena from the Duke Parapsychology Laboratory.* New York, NY: Ecco, 2009.

Jenkins, Mark. *Vampire Forensics: Uncovering the Origins of an Enduring Legend.* Washington, DC National Geographic, 2010.

Krulos, Tea. *Monster Hunters: On the Trail with Ghost Hunters, Bigfooters, Ufologists, and Other Paranormal Investigators.* Chicago, IL: Chicago Review, 2015.

Lecouteux, Claude, and Jon Graham. *The Secret History of Vampires: Their Multiple Forms and Hidden Purposes.* Rochester, VT: Inner Traditions, 2010.

Matthews, Rupert. *The Little Book of the Paranormal.* Stroud, Glouchestershire, England: History Press, 2010.

Mogk, Matt. *Everything You Ever Wanted to Know About Zombies.* New York, NY: Gallery Books, 2011.

Peck, M. Scott. *Glimpses of the Devil: A Psychiatrist's Personal Accounts of Possession, Exorcism, and Redemption*. New York, NY: Free Press, 2009.

Sherman, Aubrey. *Vampires.* Avon, MA: Adams Media, 2014.

Southall, Richard. *Haunted Route 66: Ghosts of America's Legendary Highway.* Woodbury, MN: Llewellyn Worldwide, 2013.

Straub, Peter. *Ghost Story.* New York, NY: Berkley Books, 2016.

Sugg, Richard. *Mummies, Cannibals, and Vampires: The History of Corpse Medicine From the Renaissance to the Victorians.* New York, NY: Routledge, 2011.

Index

T

U

V

W

Z